CHICAGO
TRANSIT
HIKES

D1598295

CHICAGO
TRANSIT
HIKES

A guide to getting
out in nature
without a car

By Lindsay Welbers

Printed in the United States of America
First edition 2020

ISBN: 978-1-950843-11-4

Parafine Press
3143 W. 33rd St. #6
Cleveland, OH 44109

Book design by Meredith Pangrace

For Dave, the best person I know to go tromping about in nature with.

LAND ACKNOWLEDGMENT

Chicago owes a lot to the American Indians who lived here prior to European settlement. Their names feature prominently on signs for towns and businesses, and we still use foot trails they blazed thousands of years ago as major roads. Chicago and the areas included in this book are the traditional homelands of the Council of the Three Fires: the Odawa, Ojibwe, and Potawatomi nations. Many other tribes called this area home, including the Miami, Ho-Chunk (Winnebago), Sauk, Menominee, and Fox nations. The last group of American Indians to be displaced from Chicagoland occurred after the 1833 Treaty of Chicago, signed by President Andrew Jackson. Chicago has always sat at the intersection of several great waterways, which makes it an attractive place to travel, work, live, and connect with nature. Chicago today is more diverse than ever before, and American Indians continue to call Chicago home. Today it is home to the third-largest urban American Indian community, whose members still practice its heritage and traditions. Those traditions include caring for the land, waterways, plants, and animals that also call this place home

CONTENTS

INTRODUCTION

HIKES IN CHICAGO

UNION PACIFIC NORTH

MILWAUKEE DISTRICT NORTH

UNION PACIFIC NORTHWEST

SOUTH SHORE LINE

SUGGESTED ITINERARIES

ACKNOWLEDGEMENTS

INTRODUCTION

Why take the train if I already have a car?

Let's talk about what a hike is. If I've decided that today I'm going to go hiking, I've decided two things. One, I'm going to get out into nature. Two, I'm going to take a walk. That's it. That's all that's involved.

There's no rule that says all the walking needs to be in nature for it to be a hike. Personally, I'd rather spend ninety minutes walking to and then taking the train, than walking into my garage, getting into my car, pulling out of the alley, getting onto the Edens, and paying the tolls. The whole way dozens of billboards will remind me that Brian Urlacher is not bald. If the weather is nice, I can roll down the window and breathe in the exhaust of all the other motorists while I ride the brakes to my exit. Then I'll step right out onto the trail after I pull into the parking lot. If that sounds appealing to you, put down this book and do that instead.

In Chicago we're fortunate to have a robust public transit system, which means generally a car isn't necessary. So why should one be necessary to get out into nature? With this book I aim to encourage you to shift your thinking on what a hike is. Instead of your hike beginning the moment you get to the trailhead, think that it starts the moment you walk out the front door. If you're taking the train to the trailhead, then the walk to the station is the start of your hike. Instead of a ninety-minute, frustrating drive through traffic down the expressway, you can spend that time reading a book, watching the scenery roll by or people watching. Relax in a way that's not possible when you drive a car. Heck, get up and walk around if you're feeling antsy.

The next leg of your hike is from the train station to the trailhead. Depending on where you're going this can be as easy as walking across the street, or more than a mile. I've included a mix of options in this book. The way I see it, I'd rather expend this energy checking train schedules and walking a bit further, than spend it sitting in traffic. Once you're at the trailhead, hike to your heart's content. Many parks close around sunset anyway, so that's a good time to begin moving back towards the train station.

For me, when I leave the trail after a good hike, I'm usually pretty hungry. Thankfully, train stations are typically located in the center of town, and that means you usually have a few options for refreshment. My favorite thing to do is to walk right off the trail and directly to a barstool where they'll give me a craft beer and a patty melt. Consider grabbing a bite to eat before you get on the train, so you can lull yourself into a food coma for the ride back. Have a beer if you like, because you're not driving. The time spent walking back from the trailhead to the train, and from the train back to your house is the end of your hike.

America is a car-centric country, and that makes it a bit tricky to get out into nature without one. Not impossible, just tricky. It involves a little more planning, but not much, and a little more research, which is what I'm here to help with. That said, in addition to all the ways you can use your train time, transit hiking also offers certain advantages, like free access to parks where cars pay to enter but people don't. Does your friend want to come hiking with you, but she's got to work in the morning? Why not have her hop on a train when her shift is done and meet you in the park? This book is designed to help you get out into nature, stretch your legs a bit, enjoy the outdoors around Chicago, and end your hike at your front door, without the use of a car.

How cars ruined my hike: a cautionary tale

The time I spend getting to and from the trailhead affects just everything about how I feel about the overall trip, whether I like it or not. I once left the Shawnee Forest in mid-afternoon, feeling renewed and revitalized after a few days backpacking and watching a solar eclipse from underneath totality. I left the park, pulled into the nearest gas station, and got one of those big, cold fountain drinks with those teeny, tiny ice cubes (the first cold drink I'd had in a few days of August heat). After I filled up the tank in my car, I pulled onto I-57, which I then learned was gridlock from Carbondale to Chicago. Everyone who had traveled to Southern Illinois from the north to see the eclipse now had to take the same highway back. We waited to see the end of the eclipse, but a lot of the crowd had thinned out shortly after totality. By the time we got on the road, it was bumper to bumper. I think it took over an hour just to go from one exit to the next. I'd have pulled off the interstate somewhere and camped for the night, giving traffic a full day to clear if it was possible, but I had a job interview the next morning and rescheduling wasn't an option.

It should have been a six-hour drive, where I arrived back at my apartment around 9 pm, with plenty of time to shower and sleep before the interview. What it became was a sixteen-hour slow crawl across Illinois, mostly along back roads. They weren't necessarily faster than the highway, but at least they were moving. My husband and I took turns driving while the other slept. At one point we pulled off on the side of the road in a line of cars whose drivers also needed rest, and both slept for maybe an hour. Around three or four in the morning, when the night is at its absolute darkest, a thunderstorm rolled through. Lighting crashed into nearby cornfields, blazing so bright and jarring against the darkness of everything else that you could see the lightning bolt in your vision for a minute or two after it dissipated.

I have a few very clear memories of that drive. I do remember that the only music downloaded on our phones was the entire Led Zeppelin catalog. I remember rolling through one of those no-stoplight towns in Central Illinois a few hours before dawn and seeing a closed Casey's with a parking lot full of sleeping drivers. (A bit surreal.) I remember cresting Blue Island around dawn and realizing that I was almost home. After getting to my apartment, I brought all my stuff in, showered, slept for forty-five minutes, took a rideshare to the job interview, and did not get the job. (They posted it again the next week. So that means I didn't bomb the interview, but they didn't like any of the people they interviewed, including me.) At this point I had basically been awake for twenty-eight hours. I took another rideshare home after that, and then finally I got to fall asleep.

Later, when people would ask me how the trip to see the eclipse was, I caught myself only bitching and moaning about the *Road Warrior* adventure I was on all night across the Prairie State. I wasn't remembering to mention until much later that during the eclipse the birds all collectively fall silent at the moment of totality and then two minutes later when the sun comes back, they sing morning songs in the afternoon. I didn't bring up the campfire made on the dry riverbed at the bottom of the canyon, or the fields of prairie grasses, wildflowers, butterflies, spiders, and eagles I'd been watching for days. I think it was a solid month before I even got around to Photoshopping all the pictures I had taken during the eclipse, which was half the reason I'd wanted to stay through the end.

If everyone in a car on I-57 that day had been on a train instead, not one of us would have had that Mad Max-style adventure, and we'd all have slept in our own beds that night. I do not feel that the sixteen hours I spent driving across Illinois were a great use of my time. It was exhausting and dangerous. Amtrak was running increased service to the city of Carbondale, which would have gotten me home on time, but that would have meant camping at probably Clear Springs in the Shawnee National Forest. That would have been fine, except for the fourteen-mile hike back to the trailhead, where I would hope to be able to call a rideshare (good luck with cell phone reception though) back to the train station, followed by a seven-hour ride back to Chicago. That sounds like kind of a lot, and if I missed the train I would have been stuck in Carbondale overnight. If you have something important to do the next morning, for example a job interview, then maybe that's too many moving parts for that trip to work.

That said, if Amtrak ran from Carbondale to Chicago every two or three hours, then I would have had a much better chance of sleeping in my own bed that night. At the very least, I could have snoozed on the train instead of straining myself to exhaustion to pilot a 2,000-pound V-8 engine across the backroads of Illinois. I certainly would have talked everyone's ears off about my time spent in the forest instead of my time spent stuck in traffic. I know for sure that the calm, serene feeling that I had when I left the trail that day—a feeling cultivated over two nights of sleeping among fir and oak trees and breathing fresh forest air—would have stayed with me an awful lot longer than the few hours I got to enjoy it before the stress of the drive crept in.

That is the biggest reason why I advocate for transit adjacent hiking: it's the best way that I have found to carry that collected and serene feeling for the longest amount of time after I leave the trail. Now, if Amtrak were to install a new stop in Makana, Illinois (for example), then it would be less than a two-mile walk and I could have been in Giant City State Park, which would be a heck of a lot easier than that hypothetical fourteen-mile hike and twenty-minute car ride back to Carbondale. That's why we need increased access to passenger rail services, but that's a different soapbox.

What you need

WHAT TO BRING

- Backpack
- Phone (including spare battery and charger, just in case)
- Water (Try to drink one liter per two hours you spend actively hiking.)
- Snack or lunch
- Camera (Your smartphone is also probably pretty good for this.)
- Notebook and pen (for taking notes on plants you see, personal reflection, playing tic tac toe with your train friends)
- Comfortable walking shoes
- A spare plastic bag to pick up any trash you find that may have been left behind by previous, less courteous hikers
- Sunscreen and bug spray
- The right clothes for the weather (If it's going to be cold and wet, it's a good idea to avoid cotton fabrics because they take forever to dry and aren't great insulators.)

WHAT NOT TO BRING

- Too many tech gadgets (Bring only what you need to navigate the day.)

- Weapons, including handguns (They are prohibited by law in all public parks in Illinois.)

- Anything you intend to use to vandalize stuff (Don't write your name on nature. If you carve your name or otherwise vandalize trees, rocks, bridges, or any features within Illinois parks you risk a lifetime ban from all Illinois parks and possibly thousands of dollars in fines. If you wouldn't behave that way at your sweetheart's parents' house, don't do it here.)

- More stuff than you're willing to carry all day (A too-heavy backpack will make for a miserable hike.)

- A bad attitude (Chicagoland has an astonishingly diverse landscape of prairies, savannahs, meadows, bluffs, moraines, dunes, swamps, wetlands, rivers, and lakes. If someone has told you these things are boring or too flat to be interesting, leave that notion at home and come with an open mind.)

APPS TO DOWNLOAD

- **Google Maps:** To help identify where you are and find out where you're going.

- **Ventra:** To manage your transit on CTA, Metra, and Pace.

- **South Shore Line:** To manage your tickets specifically on the South Shore Line.

- **Transit:** To determine the best route and available train schedules.

- **Lake County Forest Preserve:** Includes maps for all the parks managed by the Lake County Forest Preserve District.

- **Seek:** Download this app, snap a picture of a plant or animal you want to identify, and the algorithm will tell you what it is, if it can.

Outdoors safety

Stay on the trail: If you go off the trail you risk trampling protected plants that may not exist anywhere else in the world. If you become injured it will be much harder for rescue workers to find you, because they look on the trails first. A map will help you avoid this distress.

Know your limits: If you've got a friend who thinks a fifty-mile out-and-back hike along the entire Lakefront Trail sounds like a fun day, and you think that sounds miserable, don't do the whole thing. Do just part and turn around and head back when you're ready. Don't hike yourself to the point of dehydration or exhaustion, or you risk serious injury. Hiking is not a race and as far as I know there aren't medals for it. And if someone *is* handing out medals for it, you probably won't get one if you're dehydrated and exhausted.

Water: Bring a water bottle with you when you leave the house, fill it up at the trailhead, and drink it as you hike. Try to drink one liter of water for every two hours you spend hiking.

Dress for the weather: Hypothermia because you didn't wear enough layers is not safe. Slipping on a rock because you wore cute flats instead of sneakers is not fun. Use your noggin, dress for the environment.

Do what park officials say: Park officials don't make rules to keep you from having a good time. They make those rules because their job is to protect both the natural environment and the visitors to the park. If they tell you not to go on a path, just do as they ask.

Know what time the sun goes down: Many parks close at sunset and hiking in the dark can be dangerous. Before you arrive at the trailhead, have an idea about how much daylight is left and try get back to the trailhead before the light fades. A small, battery-powered LED flashlight can be a helpful tool if you find yourself in the woods after sunset.

Trail etiquette

- When you meet someone on the trail say hi, but there's no need to stop.

- If you find someone who needs help go ahead and help, if you feel that it's safe for you to do so. On the trail, people rely on each other a little more.

- Don't be afraid to ask for help either. If you're lost or turned around and you encounter another hiker on the trail, ask them to help you get oriented. Everyone has been there before, don't worry.

- You get bonus points for every piece of litter you pick up that another, less courteous hiker, has left behind.

Leave No Trace practices

Leave No Trace (LNT) practices guide the way we all need to approach our time in the outdoors. The idea is to leave absolutely no trace that you were ever on the trail. This helps protect the environment itself, but it also helps maintain the natural character of the landscape.

Plan and prepare: Know where you're going, what to expect, what the weather will be like, and the train schedule for the time you want to leave.

Travel and camp on durable surfaces: Staying on the trail protects the environment. Many of the places in this book have species of plants that can't be found anywhere on the planet outside of the Chicago region. If you go off the trail you risk trampling that rare plant under your foot.

Dispose of waste properly: If you packed it in, pack it out. That includes all food wrappers, bottles, and fruit cores or peels. Littering is already bad but littering on our public lands is extra-bad.

Leave what you find: Don't pick plants, even if you think you'd look good with a flower crown. If you find a neat rock, pick it up and check it out but don't take it with you. Don't leave rocks stacked in unnatural ways.

Minimize campfire impacts: Fire has lasting effects for the environment and should be controlled, especially on prairies where it's a vital part of the natural cycle. Don't start a fire except in designated fire rings, keep fires small, and put them out completely when you're done. Follow all rules for that park regarding campfires.

Respect wildlife: Here's something to try: If you're outside and you see an animal—squirrel, bird, deer, raccoon, whatever—hold out your thumb at arm's length. If your thumb covers the animal completely, you are at a safe distance. If your thumb does not cover up the animal completely, you are too close. Never feed wildlife, ever. It teaches them to be dependent on people for food and you risk injury, because an animal will bite the hand that's feeding it and that can be quite nasty.

Be considerate of other visitors: Many people come to nature to enjoy the quiet and scenic landscape, so let them do that by respecting their experience. Yield to other users on the trail and try not to make too much noise.

Share responsibly: Maybe you and your friends were able to hold a mini-photoshoot while laying down in the tallgrass prairies, and wearing crowns you wove out of foxgloves and false indigo picked while on your hike. Plus, your pal brought their drone to snap shots from otherwise impossible angles, so the pictures you managed to capture are stunning and made to be 'grammed. Except when you post those pictures, you'll be showing your audience that it's perfectly okay to trample endangered landscapes, pick flowers so they aren't there to support the wildlife, and violate rules about where aircraft are allowed. If everyone did this, we'd have fewer prairies, fewer flowers, and more annoying technology in our natural landscapes. Think about the message you send to your audience when you post pictures of your hike online and try to encourage everyone to leave our public lands better than they found them.

Difficulty rating

It's a tricky task to rate the difficulty of a hike because there are just so many factors, and everyone's definition of "difficult" is different. I'm going to use a four-star scale system to help give an idea about the levels of difficulty found in each park.

- ★ Not very difficult; flat, well-maintained trails, abundantly accessible. Stroller parents take note.

- ★★ A little more difficult; mild changes in terrain, well-maintained trails, some hills. A nice walk.

- ★★★ Moderately difficult; with rocky or challenging terrain, few amenities, and roughly maintained trails. An invigorating hike.

- ★★★★ Suitable for hikers in good physical condition; higher mileage trails with difficult terrain. Adventure seekers take note.

Transit hubs

- Millennium Station: 151 N. Michigan Ave.
- Ogilvie Transportation Center: 500 W. Madison St.
- Union Station: 225 S. Canal St.
- LaSalle Street, 414 S. LaSalle St.

Metra

What is Metra?

Metra (metrarail.com) is the big commuter transit system serving Chicago and the suburbs. It's a very different kind of train than the 'L.' Metra riders are generally commuters who live in distant suburbs and work in the city, so you don't see quite the large mix of people as you do on the CTA. It also doesn't run as frequently as the CTA, whose trains should arrive every ten minutes or less during peak hours. On the Metra peak hours might still be one train per hour. This combination of fewer stops, longer rides, and fewer trains means Metra rides tend to be a little more low-key than those on the CTA. Most of the best transit-adjacent hiking in the Chicago region is found near the Metra, so it's the main system referenced throughout this book.

What does Metra cost?

Metra calculates its fares by distance. For example: If you get on the UP-Northwest Line from where it departs at the Ogilvie Transportation Center and get off one stop later at Clybourn and Armitage, it will only cost you $4. If instead you ride all the way up to Crystal Lake, a trip that will take over an hour, it will cost $9. You can look up the fare for your specific trip by checking the most recent train schedule, which is available on

Metra's website. I have included a rough cost estimate for each hike in this book, all those are calculated from the place the train line begins in downtown Chicago. If you live near Jefferson Park on the northwest side, for example, and get on the UP-Northwest line there going up to Crystal Lake, your trip will cost less because you traveled a shorter distance.

How do I buy a ticket?

The simplest way to buy a ticket is to download the Ventra app and buy one-way tickets through there. Each Metra line and each trip has its own possible fare, so Ventra is the simplest way to pay for exactly what you need.

Many, but not all, stations have a vending machine where you can buy a ticket before boarding the train. If you don't have access to a credit or debit card, or you prefer to pay cash, you can buy a ticket at these machines or on the train from the conductor directly but, be warned: if you have access to one of these machines and instead choose to buy your ticket from the conductor, there will be a $5 surcharge attached to your fare. It's better to plan, and save some cash.

Reduced fares

- Children ages seven to eleven qualify for reduced fares. Children under seven ride free when accompanied by a fare-paying adult. One fare paying adult can bring up to three children under seven with them for free. On weekends and certain holidays, Metra offers family fares, where up to three children aged eleven and under can ride for free with each fare-paying adult.

- Students enrolled full-time in grade school or high school, and those students who are home schooled, qualify for reduced fares. Students must present a valid letter of certification from their school on school stationary, bearing the student's name with an authorized signature. Student ID cards must be displayed to the conductor.

- Senior citizens sixty-five years of age and older, passengers with disabilities, and Medicare cardholders with an RTA-issued Reduced Fare Permit also qualify for reduced fares.

- Active duty military personnel may also qualify for reduced fares, provided they present proper military identification. Military fares are only sold at Metra ticket offices or on the train directly from the conductor.

Where does Metra depart?

Metra is made up of eleven different train lines. They don't converge at any one spot so depending on which line you're on it could depart from Ogilvie Transportation Center, Union Station, LaSalle Street, or Millennium Station. If you are departing from somewhere other than downtown, use Google Maps or the Transit app to determine which station is closest to you.

What track will my train be on?

I wish I could tell you that Metra signs are clearly placed everywhere that they need to be and that they're all super legible and make the most sense. I wish I could tell you that. If you leave from one of the major transit hubs (Ogilvie, Millennium, or Union Station) there should be plenty of conductors or just people around to tell you exactly what track and which train. If you're at any other station, don't be afraid to ask for clarification from your fellow riders. Usually, it's better to bother a stranger briefly than to find yourself standing on (literally) the wrong side of the tracks when your train starts boarding. A simple "Is this the Northwest line?" or "Is this the one into Chicago?" should be enough to get your point across.

How do I board Metra?

Not all the doors to the train open at all the stations. When your train arrives, a conductor may step out onto the platform. You should go in whatever door he indicates. When you're on board, pick a car and choose a seat in either the upper or lower deck.

Metra rolls past some of the prettiest countryside, as well as stately suburbs, and has some of the best views of the skyline. It's okay to get comfy and just enjoy the view. Stow big items on the second-story rack. If the train is not crowded, you can take up two seats, just make sure to move everything to your lap or the rack when the train fills up. Don't be the last one to do it either; it's rude and your fellow riders will judge you.

Wait, what do I do with this ticket I paid for?

The conductor will come through the car and collect tickets from all the riders who boarded at that station. If you bought your tickets using the Ventra app, open the app, select "My Metra Tickets," then select the ticket you want to use and hold it up for him to see. He may ask you to tap the screen; that's just so he can tell he's looking at the app and not at a video of the little train scene.

There are conductors?

Yes. The infrastructure that Metra runs on was installed in the nineteenth century, and it's tricky to completely overhaul the basic rail technology on which the system was built. Metra has train conductors come and collect tickets in part because to add turnstiles and run Metra's ticketing system like the CTA's would involve redoing the train cars themselves, which would cost billions of dollars. Besides that, it would put the conductors out of a job, and they also play an important role of keeping the peace on the train. If someone starts getting rowdy or putting their feet on the seats, the conductor will politely ask them to correct their behavior. This is among the reasons why the Metra is such a nice place to be.

When is my stop coming up?

Metra rides can be an hour or more. I've had some very pleasant rides where I became engrossed in a good book or closed my eyes for a second and snoozed my way past my stop. Don't be me; pay more attention. The loudspeakers in the train will announce what the next stop will be as you leave each station, so listen for yours. Pull it up on Google Maps if you're unsure of where you are. You can also ask the conductor. When you're arriving at your station, gather all your things and head to the space between each car for easy disembarking.

Quiet cars

On certain cars you will see a sign featuring an image of a shushing woman. That is the quiet car. Technically, it's only the quiet car during rush hour, so if you're on it during the day don't worry too much. The quiet car is just a designated place for people to keep off their cell phones during the ride, and if they're going to have a loud conversation, they should take it to another car.

Family cars

Like the quiet car but the opposite. Family cars are available on weekends and non-rush hour weekday trains.

Restrooms

Single-occupancy restrooms are available on Metra trains, usually hidden behind a shiny, metal sliding door. They aren't in every car, but they are on all trains.

Can I drink alcohol on Metra?

Yes, you can have a drink on Metra. Alcohol and glass bottles may be prohibited on certain festival days, like the South Side Irish Parade and the Taste of Chicago, for example. And any day of the year if you behave like an unruly jerk on the Metra, conductors will exercise their right to remove you from the train and call the police if necessary. If you are intoxicated or impaired, they may refuse to let you on the train at all. Again, if you wouldn't act like that in front of your new sweetheart's parents, don't act like that on the train.

What can I bring on the Metra?

Bikes and e-scooters are permitted on weekday trains arriving in Chicago before 6:31 a.m. and after 9:30 a.m., and those departing Chicago before 3 p.m. and after 7 p.m. Bikes are allowed on all weekend trains. Bikes are stored in the ADA-accessible railcar, so if a passenger boards who needs the accessible space, bike riders may be asked to switch cars or get off the train. I've never seen this happen in person, but it's good to keep in mind that Metra cannot guarantee bikes and e-scooters a spot on the train. During festivals and special events (for example, Lollapalooza or the Taste of Chicago) they may not let bikes and e-scooters on at all. Child-size bikes are allowed but must abide by the same rules as adult-size bikes.

Metra's accessible seating areas weren't designed to store bikes, so yours will just kind of rest in an upright position. Things get tricky when it's time to get on and off the train. Let's say you get on the UP-Northwest Line where it begins at Ogilvie Transportation Center. You and one other cyclist enter the same car. If you were planning on exiting the train at Des Plaines (so you could bike along the Des Plaines River Trail to the River Trail Nature Center) and the other person is planning to ride up to Woodstock (to explore

Emricson Park and Ryder's Woods) you each want to position your bike to minimize the amount of bike-shuffling later on.

I suggest the following script:

> You: *Which station are you exiting?*
> Other rider: *Woodstock.*
> You: *Des Plaines.*

Now you know that the other rider will get off the train after you, so to simplify everyone's ride, let the other rider secure their bike on the train first. That way when you go to exit the train you won't need to wait for them to move their bike. You may need to repeat this conversation for each new biker who enters the train car throughout the ride. When I bring a bike on Metra I try not to sit too far away from my bike, just in case it needs to be moved during the ride.

One last note: If you take your bike on the Metra, bring a bungee cord with you. The conductor will require you to secure your bike so that it doesn't fall or block the passageway. The easiest way to do that is with a bungee cord that secures your bike to the seat itself, or another bike if there's already one there. If you forget your bungee, I've seen people use their locking cables, helmets, or the belt from their pants. The conductors are serious about this, so plan ahead.

Pets are permitted on weekend trains and non-peak weekday trains arriving in Chicago before 6:31 a.m. and after 9:30 a.m. and departing Chicago before 3 p.m. and after 7 p.m. That is, of course, provided your pet is small enough to fit in a carrier and can fit on your lap, under the seat, or on the overhead rack. Metra may remove passengers with pets if they are noisy or create a disturbance.

Service animals are always allowed on all Metra trains.

Oversized items can be a challenge. Metra does not check baggage and space is limited. That means, unfortunately, skis, non-folding carriages, and other large items cannot be carried. Most of the time the rule is that if you can carry that item without assistance, it can be allowed on Metra. So that cooler full of snacks and drinks for when you and all your friends get to the beach? If one of you can carry it without help, it should be fine.

Can I smoke on Metra?

No smoking is allowed on any trains, in the stations, or within fifteen feet of the station's entrances. This includes e-cigarettes and vapes.

Get there a few minutes early

Metra runs on a limited schedule, and sometimes that schedule varies. More often the train will be late rather than early, but it's a good idea to get to the station five or ten minutes before your train is scheduled to arrive. This is especially true if you're not familiar with the station you're leaving from, so you can verify which platform you want to wait on for the correct train.

If the train arrives and you're not sure if it's the one you want, the conductor will be happy to tell you.

A cautionary tale: I once thought I knew what I was doing because Google Maps said the train that I wanted was the next one, and that I was on the correct track for it. The train came and I boarded without confirming with the conductor. I sat down in my seat and began scrolling my phone for what I thought would be a ten-minute ride to Jefferson Park. After those ten minutes elapsed, I watched Jefferson Park roll right on past me without even slowing down. In fact, the train didn't stop at all for quite a while. That was the day I learned about Metra's express train. Don't be like me; check with the conductor unless you want to kill forty-five minutes waiting for the next train headed into Chicago from Arlington Heights.

CTA

What is the CTA?

The Chicago Transit Authority (transitchicago. com) operates the buses and trains that make up the circulatory system of Chicago. For this book, we're just going to focus on the trains. The trains are called the 'L,' which is official and confusing shorthand for "elevated." The CTA operates nine train lines, each named for a designated color.

What does the 'L' cost?

A full-fare ride on an 'L' train is $2.50, the reduced rate is $1.25, and the student rate is $.75. Transfers, which are for up to two additional rides within two hours, cost $.25, $.15, and $.15 accordingly. A one-day pass can be purchased at full fare for $10, a three-day pass at $20, a seven-day pass at $28, and a thirty-day CTA/Pace pass at $105 or $50. That is the only pass sold at the reduced rate.

How do I buy a ticket?

Ventra passes can be purchased from a machine in most train stations, using cash or your credit or debit card.

If you're a visitor to Chicago, go ahead and buy the multiday pass for the length of time you'll be visiting our city; it'll be cheaper in the long run.

If you're a local, or you're planning to hang around for a while, buy a Ventra card. A new one will cost $5, but you can set it to automatically reload from your bank account, if that appeals to you. Ventra readers can also accept contactless payments such as Apple Pay, Google Pay, and Samsung Pay, or any contactless bank card. Connect your Ventra card through the Ventra app and you can add value right from your phone.

Where does the 'L' go?

The 'L' is made up of 140 different stops across most of Chicago. All the train lines converge downtown and use the same tracks to navigate a small but dense square of the economic center of the city. Literally, that's why we call it the Loop. The nine different train lines extend out from downtown and act as a circulatory system for the city's residents. I suggest checking Google Maps if you're unsure where the nearest train station to you is located.

How does ticketing work?

Once your Ventra account has had money loaded into it (this will take seconds, usually), all you need to do is tap the card on the Ventra logo at the turnstiles. When the green "GO" appears, move ahead.

You can use one Ventra card to pay for the rides of up to six people. The easiest way to do that is for one person to stand on the side and tap the card on the turnstile for each person whose fare they are paying for, then going through the turnstiles last in their group.

What track will my train be on?

The answer to that varies depending on the train line, station, and neighborhood you're in. The 'L' usually has pretty good signage for where you want to go. The direction each train heads in is named for the stop where it terminates, so it helps to have a general idea of Chicago's geography. Here's a cheat sheet if you're unfamiliar with the system.

Red: Howard on the north, 95th/Dan Ryan on the south

Orange: Midway on the southwest, Loop on the east

Yellow: Howard on the south, Dempster-Skokie on the north

Green: The Loop on the east, Harlem on the west, and Ashland/63rd or Cottage Grove on the southeast

Blue: O'Hare on the northwest, through the Loop, terminating at Forest Park on the west

Purple: The Loop on the south and, depending on the time of day, either Linden or Howard on the north

Brown: The Loop on the south and Kimball on the north

Pink: The Loop on the east and 54th/Cermak on the west

How do I board the 'L'?

The signs in each station should indicate where the train will arrive when it gets there. You see those blue bumps on the edge of the platform? Stay behind those while you wait. Don't wait directly on them, you'll be too close to the train and it's dangerous. Between November and March, outdoor platforms may feature a small shelter with a heat lamp. Stand underneath this and enjoy the comfort you get from feeling like a fast food hamburger. When the train arrives, wait for everyone to finish exiting before you board. Take a seat if there's one available. If not, you'll have to stand. Move into the middle of the car and don't crowd the door. That makes it easier to fit more people into the train.

When is my stop coming up?

There should be a map above one of the doors in the car. Reference it, if you're unsure where your stop is. Politely ask someone for help if you're confused, we've all been there.

Behavior on the train

You're going to see a large mix of people on the 'L' because it's a daily utility for most Chicagoans. The best rule for how to behave on the 'L' is to mind your own business, don't take up more than one seat, move into the center of the train if its crowded, and generally try not to get in anyone's way. If we can all do that, we all usually have a pretty pleasant ride.

- Don't cross between the cars. It's dangerous and prohibited by the CTA.

- Don't vandalize any ads or any part of the train, that is also prohibited by the CTA.

- Listening to music is fine, if you have headphones.

- If you have a large backpack and the train gets crowded, take it off and put it on the floor between your feet.

Restrooms

'L' cars do not have restrooms. CTA stations by and large do not have public restrooms. Honestly, don't count on a CTA restroom facility, they just aren't there.

The CTA has expressly forbidden using the train car itself as a restroom, and you'll likely know immediately if someone has violated this rule. *Pro tip: If you see an otherwise crowded train with one oddly empty car, it's probably empty for a reason. Steer clear.*

What can I bring on the 'L'?

Just about anything if you can manage to carry it on your own, in one trip, without assistance. Don't bring anything so big it blocks the exit or the movement of other passengers.

Bikes

You can bring your bike on the 'L' train every day except during weekday rush hour (7–9:00 a.m. and 4–6:00 p.m.). Bikes are not allowed on certain days when trains are expected to be very crowded, like July 4. If a train becomes overly full, bikes may not be allowed. Up to two regular bicycles are allowed inside each train car. Folding bikes are always allowed on the train, but try not to let them take up too much floor space, okay?

Bike parking racks are installed outside most CTA rail stations, and street parking is available near almost all of them. And more than eighty stations even have indoor racks in sheltered locations. The really swank ones let you store your bike inside the station, behind the turnstiles, so it will be much less likely to get stolen while you're off adventuring. (Looking at you, Davis Street Purple Line, you beautiful thing.)

When parking your bike at a CTA station, make sure you do so in a way that still allows other cyclists to share the rack. If you leave it there for too long the CTA may declare your bike abandoned and remove it; this is really intended to be a short-term storage solution. Don't lock your bike to anything that isn't the bike rack either, or it may get removed.

Anyone fourteen years or older can bring a bike on an 'L' train, twelve- and thirteen-year-olds may with an adult accompanying them. Kids under twelve cannot bring their bikes on the train. Bikes are only allowed in the railcars with the sliding doors, not the folding ones. Let passengers board the train first; your bike goes in after they do. Priority seating is intended for seniors and customers with disabilities, so let them have those seats. Do not ride your bike inside the train station, it's dangerous.

Pets
If your pet fits in a small container designed for travel and is carried by one person, or it can fit under a seat, your pet is allowed. Service animals are also allowed.

What can I not bring on the 'L'?
All weapons including guns, clubs, knives, stun guns, tasers, and explosives are prohibited. Same

with inflammables, acids, and biohazards. In short: don't bring anything that might cause harm to yourself or others.

Can I smoke on the 'L'?
Smoking of all kinds, including e-cigarettes and vapes, is banned on CTA property. That includes within fifteen feet of all doors and entrances to stations.

Can I drink alcohol on the 'L'?
Nope, all food and drink are prohibited on the CTA.

Can I eat my lunch on the 'L'?
Nope, all food and drink are prohibited on the CTA.

South Shore Line

What is the South Shore Line?
The South Shore Line (mysouthshoreline.com) is not affiliated with Metra, CTA, or Ventra. It's its own unique passenger rail line. You can take it from Millennium Station all the way to South Bend, Indiana. In this book it will carry you primarily to Northerly Island, the Lakefront Trail, and, best of all, the Indiana Dunes. It operates in many ways exactly like Metra does.

What does the South Shore Line cost?
The South Shore Line's fare system is distance based in the same way that Metra's is.

- Reduced fares are half the full fare for a given trip. Children aged thirteen and under qualify for a reduced fare, but the conductor has the right to request proof of age.

- Students in accredited elementary, middle, and high schools qualify for a reduced one-way or twenty-five-ride ticket.

- Seniors aged sixty-five or older are eligible for a reduced fare on all trains. To qualify, present proof of age at the time of your ticket purchase.

- Passengers who display the RTA Reduced Fare Permit, NICTD Disability Identification Card, or Medicare card, are eligible for a reduced fare when the ID is shown.

- Active duty military personnel in uniform with the Uniformed Services Common Access Card may always travel at a reduced fare.

- Groups of ten or more who reserve space at least fourteen days in advance can qualify for a special group rate.

- One adult paying full fare can bring up to three kids aged thirteen and under on the South Shore Line at no additional cost. This applies only on weekend and holiday trains, and weekday trains arriving at Millennium Station after 9:30 a.m., and departing before 3:30 p.m. or after 6:30 p.m.

How do I buy a ticket?

Download the South Shore Line app to purchase the exact quantity and type of tickets you need. All stations with vending machines accept credit, debit, and RTA Transit Benefit Cards. You can also buy them directly on the train from the conductor, but there will be a $1 fee for that.

Where does it depart?

Millennium Station

What track will my train be on?

There will be signs indicating where the South Shore Line trains are boarding. Follow those signs and confirm with the conductor if you are unsure.

How do I board the South Shore Line?

In the exact same way you would on the Metra.

How does ticketing work?

In almost the exact same way it does on the Metra, except with the South Shore Line app, and not the Ventra app.

When is my stop coming up?

The South Shore Line app has a helpful train tracker feature that not only tells you where you're going but shows you where your train is in real time.

How should I behave on the train?

The same way you would on the Metra.

What can I bring?

- An electronic device—the South Shore Line has free Wi-Fi.

- Any items you bring must either fit on your lap or under your seat.

- If you're going to bring a stroller, it's advisable to bring one that collapses. South Shore Line personnel will not help you carry strollers on or off the train while your kid is in the stroller.

Can I bring my bike?

Yes, but only on select trains, at specific stations, at specific times of year. See the website for up-to-date information. Look for the cars with the bike sign on the front, those have bike racks. The conductor will not help you get your bike on the train. Space is available on a first-come-first-served basis; if a train is overcrowded, the conductor may not allow the bike on.

Can I bring an animal?
Sure, if it's a police dog, an ADA service animal, or in a carry-on travel case that sits either on your lap or under the seat. The South Shore Line takes a hard line that emotional support animals do not qualify under the ADA as service animals. Any animal that causes a significant disturbance may be asked to leave the train. Your animal is not allowed on the seats.

Can I smoke?
Nope.

Can I drink alcohol?
More or less the same rules for alcohol that apply on Metra apply on the South Shore Line. Here they may also prohibit alcohol and glass containers during major events downtown, so keep that in mind.

Divvy

Consider taking Divvy (divvybikes.com) to and from the train station, if that's an option. Divvy is a publicly owned bikeshare system available to all Chicagoans 24/7. Many Divvy docking stations are located near CTA bus and train stops, and bikes can be checked out of and returned to any station. Reduced pricing is available for low-income Chicagoans, who should totally take advantage of it. Divvys are great. I once spent an entire winter riding one of their sturdy, heavy, lumbering bikes and always felt much safer than I would on my regular summer-season road bike.

A note on maps

You may notice there aren't any maps in this book. If I had my druthers it would be chock-full of bright, rich details, and colorful maps for each park, with all hiking trails included and the train stations marked. The consequence of that is this book would be twice as long and come with a price tag to match its heft.

I've done my best to include very clear information about how to get where you are going. I suggest you double check the directions for your individual trip on Google Maps to avoid confusion or getting lost when planning your day hike. Maps for the parks can often be found near the trailhead, and many are available online for free.

If you are visiting a park that is managed by the Lake County Forest Preserve District, download the Lake County Forest Preserves District app, which is free for both Android and IOS. This app includes trail maps, news, information, and plant identification tools. *Pro tip: Snap a picture of the map on your phone when you get to the trailhead, so you'll have one to refer to in your pocket.*

HIKES IN CHICAGO

Chicago Lakefront Trail

The Lakefront Trail is the Red Line of hiking trails. Busy, varied, stunning, and it connects the city from north to south. Located wholly within the city of Chicago, it reaches as far as 71st Street on the south to Ardmore on the north. During the summer months as many as 70,000 people use the trail for relaxation or as part of their commute, every day.

To understand why the Lakefront Trail is so great, you need to understand a little bit about Chicago's history. To prepare for the 1893 Chicago World's Fair, architect Daniel Burnham was commissioned to oversee the design and construction of the exhibition. This job included more than just designing some buildings and planting a few trees. Just two decades before, the city had been almost completely destroyed by the Great Chicago Fire. In the aftermath, aid poured into the city from around the globe and Chicago had seen explosive growth during the rebuilding phase. Hosting the World's Fair was Chicago's way of saying on a global stage, "We're here, we're back, and we're stronger than ever before."

The plan was to hold the fair at Jackson Park, on Chicago's southeast side. Part of that plan involved adding rich and abundant park spaces to the otherwise, at the time, desolate lakefront. That's how Jackson Park—including Wooded Island and the Garden of the Phoenix, Midway Plaisance, and (eventually) Washington Park all came to exist.

The fair was such a tremendous success that in 1909 Burnham prepared a "Plan of Chicago," which laid out his vision for the future city. It included ambitious proposals for the lakefront and the river, some of which we still haven't implemented. Easily, two of the best ideas were that every Chicagoan should be within walking distance of a park, and that the lakefront should always be kept for public recreation and not commercial development, an idea that had the support of the business community. The 1909 plan built and expanded on his work for the fair, and he envisioned Chicago as a "Paris on the Prairie."

The Lakefront Trail passes through eighteen of Chicago's neighborhoods and provides access to green space, recreation, and the natural landscape to residents of those neighborhoods and many others.

Because the Lakefront Trail is so long, and travels through so many different parts of the city, I'm not going to recommend any particular stretch. I've seen the whole thing north to south and every corner has its unique merit. Instead, here are some notable landmarks you'll find along the way if you traverse the whole thing.

Traveling from north to south:
Foster Beach: At the north end (5600 N.) of the Lakefront Trail is Foster Beach. Here you'll find concessions, bike rentals, and restrooms. Distance swimming is common here. There is an ADA accessible beach walk. Additionally, if you've ever wanted to learn the art of trapeze, the Trapeze School of New York (5200 N.) has an outdoor studio right here on Lake Michigan in the summer months. Classes are suitable for beginners; visit chicago.trapezeschool.com for details.

Montrose Beach: (4400 N.) Chicago's largest public beach and home to rare nesting birds, including a pair of piping plovers in 2019. The beach offers soft sand, concessions, volleyball courts, and access to the clear, blue, freshwater lake. The adjacent natural habitat includes the Montrose Point Bird Sanctuary (aka the Magic Hedge), which is especially vibrant during the spring and fall migration seasons. There is also a rare panne habitat, a flat, wet, and open sandy area. Endangered plants and birds thrive in this urban oasis.

Belmont Harbor: Unless you have a boat, the Belmont Harbor itself is just something neat to look at as you pass. That said, if you're out with your favorite pooch, you will want to visit the Belmont Harbor Dog Beach (3500 N.). Especially great on a hot day, this is where you can let your furry friend off leash to chase balls in the sand and surf.

Peggy Notebaert Nature Museum: The Peggy Notebaert Nature Museum (2430 N. Cannon Dr.) is great year-round and has beautiful gardens and landscaping. The very best time to go, however, is in the winter. The high ceilings and abundant sunshine you'll find in the indoor butterfly house will instantly improve your mood in the often-gloomy Chicago winter, but even better it's always kept at a cozy 80 degrees (26 C). Take off your coat and sit in summer weather, even if outside it's subzero and sleeting. Great for families, this museum focuses on the natural history of the Chicago region.

Lincoln Park Zoo: Open year-round and free, the Lincoln Park Zoo (2001 N. Clark St.) is one of the oldest zoos in North America, and is known for its big cats, polar bears, penguins, gorillas, reptiles, and monkeys. There is also a burr oak tree that dates to 1830, a full three years before the town of Chicago was incorporated.

Lincoln Park Conservatory: Also, free and open year-round, but best in the winter. This Victorian-era glass house (2391 N. Stockton Dr.) is beautiful and full of three acres of indoor gardens and horticultural collections. This is another one of the few places in Chicago you take stroll casually without a coat in February. *Pro tip: Count the dinosaurs in the fern room.*

Alfred Caldwell Lily Pool: Outside the Conservatory just to the north and slightly hidden, you might accidentally stumble upon this important example of landscape architecture (125 E. Fullerton Parkway, between Stockton and Cannon drives.) This is one of the famed architect's most fully realized designs. It was added as a National Historic Landmark in 2006 and closes from mid-November to mid-April.

North Avenue Beach: One of Chicago's most popular beaches, it includes a unique beach house that looks like a boat stranded on the shore. From the deck of this permanently docked ocean liner (1601 N.) you'll find stellar views of downtown Chicago. Swimming, kayaking, and canoeing are popular activities here, and there is an accessible beach walk. Other amenities include refreshments, bike rentals, yoga, open-air sports, lake boarding, lounge chairs, jet skis, volleyball, restrooms, and ATMs. Distance swimming is available at the north end of the boathouse.

Oak Street Beach: Running alongside the posh Gold Coast neighborhood this stretch (1550-500 N.) includes a wide, sandy swimming beach and a wide, sloped, concrete path around the Oak Street Curve of Lake Shore Drive that leads to a set of ledges where spectators often watch distance swimming competitions. Swimmers enter the water at the Ohio Street Beach to the south. *Pro tip: The Oak Street Curve portion of the trail can be quite dangerous depending on conditions; it's recommended to avoid this spot if the waves are high. I'm speaking from terrifying personal experience here.*

Ohio Street Beach: Within walking distance of Navy Pier, Ohio Street Beach (600 N.) has concessions, bike rentals, watersports rentals, restrooms, and a lifeguard first aid station. It is not recommended to swim if a lifeguard is not on duty, so keep that in mind.

Navy Pier Flyover: Constructed to help alleviate congestion when traveling over the river, the Navy Pier Flyover is an elevated biking and walking path. The most useful section of the flyover opened in 2019 and goes over Grand Avenue and Illinois Street, making it easier for people traveling on foot or bicycle to avoid mixing with traffic. The remaining portions of the flyover are currently expected to open in 2020.

Maggie Daley Park: Opened in 2015 Maggie Daley Park (337 E. Randolph St.) is a public park named after the late wife of former Mayor Richard M. Daley, and features a fieldhouse, ice skating ribbon, climbing walls, notable landscaping, and a modern, wholly accessible and supremely cool children's playground. Stroller families, take note.

Grant Park: Long considered Chicago's front lawn, Grant Park bumps right up against the heart of downtown, Maggie Daley Park, the Lakefront Trail, and the Museum Campus. Notable landmarks include Millennium Park (that's where you'll find the Bean, aka Anish Kapoor's Cloud Gate sculpture), Buckingham Fountain, Frank Gehry's swooping Pritzker Pavilion, the Petrillo Music Shell, manicured gardens, ice skating rinks, a skate park, and a dog park, as well as lots more public art.

Museum Campus: This peninsula jutting out into Lake Michigan is where we keep our major cultural institutions including the Adler Planetarium, the Field Museum of Natural History, the Shedd Aquarium, and Soldier Field (where the Bears play).

Northerly Island: A peninsula-off-a-peninsula, this island has its own fascinating and dodgy political history and is absolutely worth its own tour. See Northerly Island chapter for the scoop.

31st Street Beach: Named in honor of noted Chicagoan Margaret T. Burroughs, artist and founder of the DuSable Museum of African American History.

This public beach (3100 S.) has excellent swimming, skyline views, an accessible playground, concessions, and restrooms.

49th Street Beach, Morgan Shoal, and Shipwreck of the Silver Spray: The Morgan Shoal is a limestone reef that extends for about half a mile into Lake Michigan from this point. And if the water levels are low, you might spy the pointed nose of a sunken ship off the coast of 49th St. In 1914 the Silver Spray, a passenger ferry, ran aground of the Morgan Shoal and sank over the course of three days. No one was injured but also no vessel was able to pull boat free of the limestone reef below. Eventually, waves broke the boat apart while rubberneckers watched from the beach. Today, you can still sometimes see it peek out from the water as you stand on the tiny, rocky, beach. Adventurous swimmers will snorkel or even scuba the shipwreck from this beach. If you're more inclined to stay on land, fossils frequently wash up here.

Promontory Point: This man-made peninsula (5400 S.) juts into Lake Michigan and consists of huge limestone blocks arranged in a series of four steps leading to a promenade. Swimming is very popular here. This is one of the few locations in the city where parkgoers can build a fire in designated fire pits. Public restrooms are available in a building that resembles a tiny castle. The city controversially closed the Point to the public in 2013 for the lavish wedding reception of filmmaker George Lucas and Mellody Hobson.

Museum of Science and Industry: This imposing museum (5700 S.) is the only remaining structure left on the site of the 1893 Chicago World's Fair. Today it's a world-renowned science and technology museum that sits at the north end of Jackson Park. It is worth a visit for kids and adults of any age.

Jackson Park, the Garden of the Phoenix, and Wooded Island, plus someday the Obama Presidential Center: Jackson Park (6400 S.) has a long and storied history. Wooded Island came to exist because every delegation from every nation that visited the 1893 World's Fair donated a tree to the city, and they were planted here on this island. The Garden of the Phoenix was a gift from the Japanese delegation and offers one of the most serene environments for quiet reflection in Chicago. Notable changes since the fair include The Darrow Bridge, named in honor of Clarence Darrow, whose ghost they say haunts it, and *Skylanding*, a sculpture installation by Yoko Ono. The Obama Presidential Center, in the works for four years and counting, is slated to be built in the park, though at press time no groundbreaking date had been set.

South Shore Cultural Center: The South Shore Cultural Center (7100 S.) has a story that mirrors the neighborhood and not always in the most flattering ways. Built as a country club for wealthy Protestants in 1905, the club later became more inclusive when Irish-Catholics were admitted. In 1967 the club considered opening its doors to African Americans and Jewish people, but members voted against it. Which, side eye. By 1973 the club had liquidated its assets and sold the building to the Park District. Today it is a beautiful example of Mediterranean Revival architecture and a vital cultural resource for Chicagoans of all backgrounds. It has a public beach, protected nature preserves, and a nine-hole golf course that is open to the public. If you remember the scene in *The Blues Brothers* where they play a raucous concert in the Palace Hotel Ballroom, that was filmed here. Also, it's where Barack and Michelle Obama had their wedding reception.

Rainbow Beach: The Lakefront Trail terminates at 71st St., or the north end of Rainbow Beach, which extends further south to 79th St. Rainbow Beach has a gymnasium, fitness center, community garden, restrooms, sport courts, baseball diamonds, and playgrounds. Breathtaking views of Lake Michigan and Downtown Chicago can be seen from the fieldhouse. The soft sand beach is stunning and has probably the singular best views of Chicago's skyline that you'll find, though it will feel a world away.

Park name	Chicago Lakefront Trail
Train station	Too many to list.
Train line	Metra: UP-North, UP-Northwest CTA: Blue, Brown, Red lines
Schedule	Depending on the train line, any time day or night.
Trail access	There are many, many ways to access the Lakefront Trail. I could try to list them all, but someone will undoubtedly correct me. **Good CTA options include:** Cermak-McCormick Place (Green Line), Roosevelt* (Red, Orange, Green lines), Adams/Wabash* (Brown, Purple, Orange, Green, Pink lines), Washington/Wabash (Brown, Purple, Orange, Green, Pink lines), Grand,* Chicago, Fullerton,* Belmont, Addison, Sheridan, Wilson,* Lawrence, Argyle, Berwyn, Bryn Mawr (Red and Purple lines), Lake, Monroe, Jackson (Red Line), Armitage,* Diversey, Wellington (Brown Line), Washington, Monroe, Jackson (Blue Line) **Good Metra options include:** Metra Electric South Chicago Branch: Cheltenham, South Chicago Branch and the South Shore Line*: 63rd Street, University of Chicago/59th St., 55th-56th-57th St., 51st/53rd St.*, Kenwood/47th St., 27th Street, Metra Electric to University Park Branch: Museum Campus/11th St.*, Millennium Station*, UP North: Ravenswood
Hours	The lakefront trail is open 24 hours a day, but the parks surrounding it close between 11 p.m. and 6 a.m. daily.
Miles of trails	18.5
Difficulty	✶ — ✶✶✶
In-park recreation options	Walking, jogging, in-line skating, bicycling, skateboarding, dog park, ice skating, kiteboarding (Montrose Beach only), canoeing, kayaking, fishing, birding, picnicking, art appreciation

Amenities	Restrooms, concessions, museums, ice skating, public art, restaurants, beaches, playgrounds. This trail goes through 18 neighborhoods and downtown Chicago. If there's an outdoor activity you want to do, you can probably find it somewhere along this trail.
Safety concerns	Lake Michigan is the largest freshwater lake within a single country that exists anywhere on earth. When water is high and weather is rough, it is a powerful force of nature. If winds or water are high, Lake Michigan may become a hazard and the Park District may close the path. If this happens, just stay away. They don't call it a Great Lake for nothin'.
	This trail is also a popular trail with commuters. As a result, the pace of things on this trail is a little more varied than you might find out in a remote nature preserve. Consider this to be an active hike and follow the painted path instructions.
	• Pedestrians have the right of way.
	• Slower traffic stays to the right.
	• Wear protective gear while biking or skating.
	• At night, wear highly visible, reflective materials.
	• Signal to others and always pass on the left.
	• Before entering the trail, look both ways and yield to oncoming traffic.
	• If you need to stop for any reason, do so on the side of the trail, allowing others to proceed.
	• Don't bike or skate while wearing headphones or under the influence of alcohol.
Water	Lake Michigan runs to the east of all 18.5 miles of this trail. It's a beautiful and magnificent force of nature, so try to treat it with respect.
Accessibility	This path is paved, wide, and largely flat. There are only few steep slopes, and it is largely very ADA-compliant. Much of the trail includes separate bike and walking paths.
Dogs	Yes—on leashes only
Bikes	Yes—this park is very bike friendly
Family-friendly	Yes, but be aware that slower travelers should stay on the right-hand side of the path.

Museum Campus/11ᵗʰ Street: Northerly Island Park

There is so much Chicago history in this little island. Some of it great, some of it corrupt as all get-out.

Northerly Island is a man-made peninsula jutting off Chicago's shoreline, just south of the Museum Campus. It was built as part of Daniel Burnham's 1909 "Plan of Chicago," which called for a lakefront park as part of a five-island chain between Jackson Park and 12th St. The other four islands were never built. Burnham wanted Northerly Island covered in trees and grasses for public enjoyment, which is pretty on-brand for that guy. He died in 1912, and the man who co-authored the plan, Edward H. Bennett, re-wrote it in 1916 to say the island would be better suited for an airport, instead of public enjoyment. Which, hmmm.

In 1920 Chicago voters approved a $20 million bond ($267,327,461.14 by 2020 dollars) to create the island and construction was completed in 1925. The Great Depression and World War II kept it from opening as an airport until 1946.

In 1933-34 the island was the hub of activity for the Century of Progress World's Fair. As part of the exposition, twenty-four Italian Savoia-Marchetti S55X flying boats made their first transatlantic formation flight between Italy and Chicago. The flyers were under the command of General Italo Balbo. He was greeted as a dignitary and his visit was commemorated when the City of Chicago named Balbo Avenue after him. Today, some would like to see the street renamed, due to Balbo's close association with fascist leader Benito Mussolini.

In 1938 the Works Progress Administration connected the island to the mainland via a causeway at 12th St. Up until this time Northerly Island had been full of paths, walkways, and a beach. In 1946 the Illinois legislature deeded twenty-four acres of adjacent lake bottom to Chicago, to create additional landfill, to make a runway of adequate length. Named Meigs Field, the airport began receiving airplanes on this single strip in the middle of Lake Michigan in December 1948. By 1955 it was the busiest single-strip airport in the United States. In the 1970s it became a vital resource for aeromedical transport of patients and transplant organs, when that technology got useful. Corporate aircraft were frequent and heavy users of the airport. Commuter airline service peaked in the 1980s, but regional service was offered by carriers including Illini Airlines, Ozark Air Lines, Midwest Commuter Airways, and Skystream Airlines. President John F. Kennedy landed at Meigs Field when visiting Chicago to avoid inconveniencing regular travelers.

On October 15, 1992 a Boeing 727-100 jetliner made its final landing at Meigs Field. United Airlines donated the jet, which was at the end of its usable life, to the Museum of Science and Industry to become an exhibit. Meigs at the time had a 3,900-foot runway, well short of the length such a plane normally used, but it was lightly loaded, and it set down without issue. The jet was then loaded onto a barge and sailed south down Chicago's coastline to the museum at 57th St. To get it into the museum involved removing limestone columns from the historic building and taking off one of the jet's wings (which didn't fit inside the Great Hall). There's a video of this tremendous engineering feat you can watch if you visit the Museum of Science and Industry.

In the early 1990s, Chicago-area Tuskegee Airmen, Inc., provided free airplane rides and aviation education to Chicago youth at Meigs Field. Thousands of children took their first airplane ride or became exposed to the aviation industry through this program until 2003.

This entire time the land was owned by the Chicago Park District. Which if you stop and think about it for a second, it's ridiculous that the Park District would manage an airport. In 1994 Mayor Richard M. Daley declared his plan to close the airport and build a park in its place. In 1996, the Park District refused to renew the lease for the airport, and from October 1996 to February 1997, Meigs Field actually closed, until pressure from the state legislature persuaded the city to reopen it to air traffic.

In 2001 a compromise between Chicago, the State of Illinois, and other involved parties would have kept the airport open for another twenty-five years. However, the federal part of the deal didn't pass the United States Senate.

So, in a controversial, illegal, and politically popular move, in the middle of the night on March 30, 2003 Mayor Daley had city crews destroy the airport by bulldozing gigantic X-shaped gouges across the runway. Sixteen planes were left stranded on the ground, and one in flight had to be rerouted.

At a news conference the next morning Mayor Daley declared, "To do this any other way would have been needlessly contentious." One aviation interest group called his actions "appalling," while the Chicago Tribune editorial board tutted, and its columnists tsked. Interest groups attempted to get the airport reopened but were unsuccessful. The Federal Aviation Administration ultimately fined the city of Chicago for not giving the required thirty-days' notice before closing an airport. The fine was the maximum allowed under the law at the time: $33,000.

However, conservationists and regular Chicagoans who don't usually take private airplanes and do visit parks heralded the move. Was it democratic or fair? Eh, maybe not. Did Chicago need more greenspace than it needed a tiny private airport in the middle of the lake? Undoubtedly yes. Besides, the site was always intended to be a park. Environmentalists were ready with an urban wilderness plan, and by August that year Northerly Island was re-opened as a public park.

In 2006 the city agreed to pay the FAA's fine, plus repay the $1 million in misappropriated FAA Airport

Improvement Program Funds that were used to destroy the airfield and build the park. That's the best part of this story, for me. That in the dead of night Hizzoner Mayor Richard M. Daley dipped into the Airport Improvement Fund to improve the airport by destroying it, because the fine for that was cheaper than the cost of the lawyers needed to take it through court. Oh, Chicago.

Today, this ninety-one-acre island is a public park with prairie grasses, strolling paths, a 7,500-seat pavilion, and a beach. The city planted 11,000 shrubs and 400 trees. Visitors will find no shortage of neoclassical and modern sculptures, a visitor's center, a courtyard, and a play space for kids. Visiting this park allows for a lovely stroll in a beautiful landscape, filled with birds, especially during migration seasons. If you enjoy watching boats sail past, this is also a great place to sit during the summer months when the harbor is busy. Year-round programming for all ages is available and often free to city residents.

The Chicago Park District has a twenty- to thirty-year framework for restoring and completing Northerly Island, including a plan to build a reef, which will provide much-needed support and protection for the wildlife in Lake Michigan. The plan is to revitalize the environment on the island by letting as much of it as possible go wild. Today, monarch butterflies and herons call it home during the summer months.

The park provides year-round programming with environmental education themes, and in winter hosts regular Polar Adventure Days intended to get parents and kids outdoors to experience nature in a way that isn't normally possible in an urban environment. On these days the Park District rents snowshoes and cross-country skis, assuming there are at least three inches of snow on the ground.

Park name	Northerly Island Park
Train station	Museum Campus/11th St.
Train line	Metra Electric District
Schedule	Monday–Friday: departs downtown Chicago as early as 5:15 a.m.; departs Museum Campus/11th St. as late as 12:41 a.m. Saturday and Sunday: departs downtown Chicago as early as 4:40 a.m. and departs Museum Campus/11th St. as late as 12:40 a.m.
Departs from	Millennium Station
Round-trip travel costs	$8 full fare, $4 reduced fare
Entrance	From the Museum Campus/11th Street Metra station head east, in the direction of Lake Michigan, and follow the path. The first big building in front of you will be the Field Museum; keep it on your right side and walk towards the Shedd Aquarium. Walk between these two buildings, and take a right onto East Solidarity Drive, heading in the direction of the Adler Planetarium. When you get to the Adler, turn around and enjoy one of the best views of Chicago's skyline that exist anywhere. Continue walking around the Adler and the entrance to Northerly Island Park will be directly ahead of you.
Hours	6 a.m. to 11 p.m. daily Bring a flashlight if you will be here after dark.
Distance from station to trailhead	The tour around the museum campus is a little over one mile.
Miles of trails	About 1, paved
Acres	91
Difficulty	★★

In-park recreation options	Hiking, walking, birding, concerts, cultural events, natural interpretive events, occasional camping for kids and families
Amenities	Beach access, sculptures
Safety concerns	This park does not have any overhead lighting, so it will get dark quickly once the sun goes down.
Plants	Much of the land here has been restored to prairie.
Water	Lake Michigan on the east and Burnham Harbor on the west.
Accessibility	The paths are wide, flat, and paved.
Admission	Free, though some events have associated costs
Dogs	No, sorry.
Bikes	Yes—this park is very bike friendly.
Family-friendly	Very, especially during the winter.
Nearby restaurants	There are a few food trucks that can be found on the Museum Campus, but otherwise there aren't many nearby.

The 606 and the Bloomingdale Trail

You know how a lot of people never quit calling it the Sears Tower mostly because Willis Tower just doesn't have that same ring to it? That's how I feel about the Bloomingdale Trail, part of a system of parks more broadly called the 606. I also sincerely feel this is among the best parks in Chicago.

Before it was a park, the trail was where the tracks for BNSF trains ran alongside Bloomingdale Avenue. In the 1990s, BNSF ceased operations along the line and the neighbors began a decade-long effort to turn the abandoned tracks into a park. Through an extensive community-focused design process, and with the work of dozens of public and civic organizations, and the eventual backing of then-Mayor Rahm Emanuel, the 606—comprising both the elevated trail and a network of street-level parks—opened in 2015. Today, at any time of day, you'll see all kinds of Chicagoans using it for recreation or as part of their commute.

The less-than three-mile-long Bloomingdale Trail has sixteen access points, plus amphitheaters, meeting spaces, seating to watch the traffic go by on Humboldt Boulevard below, public art, and opportunities for stargazing. If you've ever wanted to learn more about the specific plants that you see in Chicago parks, the Bloomingdale Trail regularly offers specialized programming on just that topic. This park is intended to be a place of education, as well as recreation and transit.

Fun fact: This park has given scientists a valuable new tool for studying microclimates in Chicago. A microclimate is the climate of a very small or restricted area, especially when it differs from the climate of the surrounding area. Chicago is a geographically large place and as we commonly hear in the weather report it's often cooler by the lake than it is out near O'Hare. Another way to say this is that Lake Michigan has a unique and strong effect on everything around it. The 606 runs east to west, which means that the further towards the western end of the park you get, the less effect Lake Michigan has on the climate where you are standing. You'll often see citizen scientists, and those from institutions like the Field Museum and the Peggy Notebart Nature Museum, out here recording data about plant and critter behavior.

Visit during the springtime to see for yourself how these changes in microclimates play out. Flowers and trees begin to bud and bloom on the western end of the park days or weeks before the same plants do their thing on the eastern end. Scientists also study how these changes in microclimates affect insects, birds and other animals.

This park was intended to be a model for all parks created in the twenty-first century. All the plants in this park were chosen because they are native to the landscape or beneficial to humans or animals. Personally, the stand of birch trees towards the western end is my favorite spot along the trail. I'm genuinely looking forward to visiting this park again and again as they grow and become denser and more mature.

Depending on the time of day and time of year you visit the Bloomingdale Trail, it can be a bit crowded. It's a wonderful park and it deserves every accolade anyone wants to give it, but it is also a transportation corridor and very popular with commuters, especially on bikes, so during morning and evening rush hour be aware. A springy blue strip along either side of the path gives walkers a low-impact cushion under their feet. Walkers are encouraged to stay on that cushioned strip, and give bikers, skaters, and runners the opportunity to pass on the left. Divvy bikes are conveniently located at various trail access points, and it's a great place to try one out in a long and car-free space.

Park name	The 606 and the Bloomingdale Trail
Train station	Damen, Western Blue line stops Clybourn Metra Healy Metra
Train line	CTA: Blue Line Metra: UP-Northwest, Milwaukee District North
Schedule	The Blue Line runs 24 hours a day, 7 days per week. Clybourn Metra: Monday–Friday: departs downtown Chicago as early as 5:42a.m. and departs Clybourn as late as 1:11 a.m. Saturday: departs downtown Chicago as early as 6:35 a.m. and departs Clybourn as late as 11:47 p.m. Sunday: departs downtown as early as 10:35 a.m. and departs Clybourn as late as 11:28 p.m. Healy Metra: Monday–Friday: departs downtown as early as 6:25 a.m. and departs Healy as late as 11:47 p.m. Saturday: Departs downtown as early as 8:35 a.m. and departs Healy as late as 11:39 p.m. Sunday: departs Chicago as early as 8:35 a.m. and departs Healy as late as 11:39 p.m.
Departs from	Ogilvie Transportation Center, Union Station, CTA Blue Line
Round-trip travel costs	Blue Line: $5, assuming the hike lasts more than two hours UP-NW: $8 full fare, $4 reduced Milwaukee District North: $8.50 full fare, $4.25 reduced.
Entrance	From the Clybourn Metra station, exit and head south on Ashland Avenue. As you exit from underneath the highway above you, the entrance to the 606 will be on your right. From the Healy Metra station head east on Fullerton Avenue, take a right onto Avers Avenue, pass through Mozart Park, take a left on Armitage Avenue and a right on Ridgeway Avenue. The trail will be ahead of you after you pass the YMCA.

	From the Damen Blue Line station, walk north up Damen for 2 blocks; the entrance to the park is directly ahead of you. From the Western Blue Line station, head south on Western Avenue for 4 blocks, the entrance to the park will be directly ahead of you. Other Blue Line stops (California, Logan Square) will also get you near the trail, but it'll be a longer walk.
Hours	6 a.m. to 11 p.m.
Distance from station to trailhead	From Clybourn Metra: Less than 1,000 feet From Healy Metra: About 1 mile From Damen Blue Line: About .25 miles From Western Blue Line: About .5 miles
Miles of trails	2.7
Acres	99
Difficulty	★★
In-park recreation options	Hiking, walking, biking, in-line skating, skateboarding, art appreciation, music, birdwatching, people watching
Amenities	Few; restrooms are not readily available on this trail.
Safety concerns	Slower traffic stays to the right, please.
Accessibility	The path is paved throughout, with a softer rubber surface on the outside edge for walkers. There a few are gravel paved paths that run alongside the main path, which can feel a little more natural. Path access is via ramps.
Dogs	Yes—on leashes only
Bikes	Yes—this park is very bike-friendly
Family-friendly	Yes, but be aware that slower travelers should stay on the right-hand side of the path.
Nearby restaurants	Many; this trail takes you directly through four of Chicago's most vibrant neighborhoods.

Conservatory Green Line: Garfield Park Conservatory

To stave off rickets and the winter blues, every Chicagoan is required to visit the Garfield Park Conservatory at least once between November and April. (I think that was a law passed under one of the Mayors Daley.)

Designed by noted architect Jens Jensen and built in 1906, this glass building is more than just a cultural institution, it's a port in a storm. Winter in Chicago can be miserable—long, cold, and uniformly gray for weeks on end—but not here. Every day of the year the conservatory has vibrant foliage, two indoor acres to meander, and temperatures above seventy-five degrees.

The Palm Room has more than seventy palms from warm habitats from across the globe; the Fern Room feels like a step back to prehistoric times. If you're a fan of houseplants, check out the Desert House (if you like jades and cacti) or the Aroid House (if you keep philodendrons and lilies). The Show House is often full of technologically creative art installations, and the indoor children's garden offers hands-on understanding of a how a plant works. Particularly good for families with kids who like to touch everything, there is a children's indoor garden that allows them to do exactly that. *Pro tip: Try to spot the axolotl. You'll find it near the sensitive plants.*

Walking through each room offers a tangibly different feeling. The Palm Room is warm and humid, the Fern Room is cooler and damp, and walking into the Desert House is like being transported halfway across the country in just a few feet. This conservatory frequently has rare and interesting plants and gives regular people the chance to see these things up close. In 2012 a rare double coconut seed briefly sprouted, giving scientists and regular folks the chance to check out an extremely rare event before the sprout died. In 2016 visitors could check out a pungent corpse flower as it bloomed over twenty-four hours. In 2019 an agave plant grew so tall they had to open space in the ceiling to let it out.

A visit during the summer months will give you access to the ten acres of gardens including the City Garden, the Sensory Garden, a labyrinth, and a lively bee colony.

Park name	Garfield Park Conservatory
Train station	Conservatory—Central Park Drive Note: You want the Conservatory stop, not the Garfield Green Line stop; that will take you to a different neighborhood.
Train line	CTA: Green Line
Schedule	Monday–Friday: the Green Line stops at the Conservatory stop as early as 4:13 a.m. and the last train exits the station around 1:42 a.m. Most of the day you can expect a train to arrive every 7 to 12 minutes. Saturday: the Green Line stops at the Conservatory stop as early as 5:13 a.m. and the last train departs las late as 1:42 a.m. Most of the day you can expect a train to arrive every 10 to 12 minutes. Sunday: the train arrives as early as 5:13 a.m. and departs as late as 1:42 a.m. You can expect a train to arrive every 12 minutes.
Round-trip travel costs	$5 full fare, $2.50 reduced
Entrance	Exit the Green Line on the north side of the street and the Garfield Park Conservatory will be directly in front of you.
Hours	The conservatory is open daily from 9 a.m. to 5 p.m., except on Wednesdays when it stays open until 8 p.m.
Distance from station to trailhead	Less than 1 block

Acres	2 in the conservatory; 10 outdoors
Difficulty	★
In-park recreation options	Walking, nature viewing, interpretive programs
Amenities	Restrooms, gift shop
Safety concerns	Not really, just make sure your shoes are tied and watch where you're going.
Plants	The Garfield Park Conservatory has more than 2,000 plant species, in 8 indoor show houses and a 10-acre outdoor garden.
Water	Decorative and practical fountains are placed throughout the conservatory and they're quite pleasant. Check out the koi in the Aroid House.
Geology	Don't miss the cooler and dryer Desert House if neat rocks are your thing.
Accessibility	The conservatory is wheelchair accessible, except the Fern Room. A limited number of free wheelchairs are available on a first-come, first-served basis.
Admission	Free, but they do accept donations.
Dogs	Service animals only
Bikes	Bikes are not allowed inside the conservatory, but ample bike parking is available outside.
Family-friendly	Yes, bring the kids to this one.
Nearby restaurants	Inspiration Kitchens, 3504 W. Lake St., is just a short walk from the conservatory and Green Line station and offers excellent food prepared by neighborhood residents.

Rosemont Blue Line: Des Plaines River Trail, Catherine Chevalier Woods, and Chippewa Woods

Enter the park after walking from the Rosemont Blue Line station and head south to enjoy Robinson Woods and Catherine Chevalier Woods.

Catherine Chevalier Woods to the south is a stunning example of a natural area with gorgeous woodlands. The meadows that make up the central part of the park here are either mowed, for picnicking and recreation, or left unmowed. Where it's unmowed you'll find prairie vegetation, oak and hickory woods, and flowers throughout the season. Native plants including anemone, toothwort, and spring beauties can be found in the warmer months, while a winter visit might give you the best chance to spot a deer. Just north of Lawrence Ave. off of River Rd. you will find an American Indian cemetery that includes the grave of Alexander Robinson, also known as Chief Chee-Chee-Pin-Quay (Chief of the Potawatomi, Chippewa and Ottawa tribes). He is laid to rest here with the members of his family. Robinson Woods south of Lawrence Ave. is named in his honor. Robinson Woods includes scattered remnant prairies and it is a popular spot for migratory birds. Beaver, turtles and mallards can be spotted along the river here.

If you head north towards Dam No. 4 Woods, instead of south when you first enter, you'll find the hiking has a little more varied terrain. North of that you'll come to Chippewa Woods and Axehead Lake. Here you'll find year-round fishing. It's one of the rare spots in Chicago where ice fishing is allowed. Not into fishing? Sit by the shore of the lake to see some of the best and most diverse birding on the west side of Chicago.

Park name	Catherine Chevalier Woods and Chippewa Woods
Train station	Rosemont
Train line	CTA: Blue Line
Schedule	The Blue Line runs 24 hours a day, 7 days per week.
Departs from	O'Hare, downtown, or Forest Park
Round-trip travel costs	$5 full fare, $2.50 reduced
Entrance	From the Blue Line take a right (heading north) onto Des Plaines River Rd. Take a right onto E. Devon Ave., cross the Des Plaines river and the entrance to the trail should be ahead of you on the right.
Hours	Sunrise to sunset
Distance from station to trailhead	About 1 mile
Miles of trails	The Des Plaines River Trail has about 30 miles of continuous trail.
Acres	The Des Plaines River Trail includes about 13,000 acres of vegetation, wetlands, and paths.
Difficulty	★★
In-park recreation options	Hiking, picnicking, biking, cross-country skiing
Amenities	Picnic areas
Safety concerns	The Des Plaines River Trail currently breaks for the Union Pacific Railroad crossing between Golf Rd. and Central Ave. Crossing is prohibited for safety reasons. The Forest Preserves of Cook County has plans to build a footbridge

	here, but a completion date is not set. Since you cannot safely cross the river at this level, cross via the pedestrian crosswalk at Bender and Golf roads. You will be able to rejoin the trail on the other side.
	Seasonal flooding is common in the sections of the path between Touhy and North avenues. Depending on the weather and conditions parts of the trail, particularly underpasses, may have standing water.
Water	This trail runs alongside the Des Plaines River, which means that flooding can be a concern.
Accessibility	The trail is stone, generally flat, and does not include any stairs or steep elements. However, it can have encroachment by vegetation that can leave it with less than the standard 10' width. There can also be roots or other small obstacles.
Dogs	Yes—on leashes only
Bikes	Yes—this park is very bike friendly.
Nearby restaurants	There's no shortage of restaurants, bars, bakeries and cafes along River Rd. Steakhouses are abundant here, but you'll also find pizza, bakeries, breweries, and taco joints.

UNION PACIFIC
NORTH

Hubbard Woods:
Skokie Lagoons

The walk between the Hubbard Woods Metra station to the Skokie Lagoons is a pleasant stroll through a pretty residential area, with beautiful architecture. When you enter the park, you will be at a scenic spot between two lagoons. Follow the path to the right and take the approximately four-and-a-half-mile loop around the northern lagoons. If you're looking for a longer hike, follow the path to the left and you will be able to access fifteen miles of out-and-back trails headed south.

The Potawatomi named this place Chewbab Skokie, which meant "Big Wet Prairie" or "Skokie Marsh," depending on who you ask. During European settlement, farmers drained it, leaving a peat bog. During spring floods, it became a lake that caused problems for the adjacent property and roads. Between 1933 and 1940, the Civilian Conservation Corps brought the waters under control by moving four million yards of earth to recontour the land. This created the artificial lagoons of today. The Forest Preserve District of Cook County will tell you that "the massive effort was the largest CCC project in the nation."

In the 1990s, the Chicago Audubon Society began a shoreline restoration project that added thousands of plants and limited erosion. Restoration efforts focused on the upstream lagoons, which helped stop erosion on the downstream lagoons. Invasive species were cleared and replaced with native plants and grasses. Today you will find goldenrod, tall coreopsis, compass plant, cup plant, aster, coneflower, switchgrass, rattlesnake masters, woodland brome, and cinquefoil. Mallards, great blue herons, white herons, finches, cardinals and blue jays are just some of the birds that can be spotted here.

Previously, aquatic herbicides were used to improve shore fishing. This included poisoning and restocking the fish and building a boat launch south of Tower Rd.

Today the Illinois Environmental Protection Agency does not advise eating the fish you catch in these lagoons. However, if you just want to catch and release, you'll find bass, walleye, northern pike, channel catfish, bluegill, crappie, and bullheads.

The waters are only about ten feet deep, which makes them ideal for kayaking, canoeing, and rowing. Boat rentals are available seasonally through Chicago River Canoe and Kayak at Tower Rd.

Visit on a cold winter day and you might hear the ice quaking. The shallow waters here mean the lagoon freezes earlier and at a lower temperature than a larger, deeper body of water might. Ice quakes happen when the air above the water drops suddenly in temperature, the cool air can penetrate down to the still-liquid water beneath the bottom of the lagoon. When that happens that still-liquid water may freeze rapidly, causing the surrounding soil to expand suddenly. When it happens in Lake Michigan it creates a loud booming sound; on a smaller body of water like this it's almost like a low-pitched squeak.

Park name	Skokie Lagoons
Train station	Hubbard Woods
Train line	Metra: Union Pacific North
Schedule	Monday–Friday: departs Chicago as early as 5:42 a.m., and departs Hubbard Woods as late as 12:40 a.m Saturday: departs Chicago as early as 6:35 a.m., departs Hubbard Woods as late as 11:15 p.m. Sunday: departs Chicago as early as 10:35 a.m. and departs Hubbard Woods as late as 10:45 p.m.
Departs from	Ogilvie Transportation Center

Round-trip travel costs	$12.50 full fare, $6.25 reduced
Entrance	From the Hubbard Woods Metra station head left on Green Bay Rd. and take a left onto Tower Rd. Follow Tower Rd. for about 1 mile and you will be in the park. There are sidewalks all along this path.
Hours	Sunrise to sunset
Distance from station to trailhead	About 1.25 miles.
Miles of trails	About 6 around the park, with access to another 15 more along the North Branch Trail System.
Acres	894, of which 190 are water
Difficulty	★★★
In-park recreation options	Hiking, biking, kayaking, canoeing, row boating, birding, fishing
Amenities	Portable bathrooms (seasonally), picnic shelters Boat rentals along Tower Rd. from May through October
Safety concerns	If the weather has been very wet the trails closer to the water can become slick and mushy surface use caution so you don't fall in.
Accessibility	The path is wide, flat, and paved. Smaller footpaths closer to the water exist in places, but they are roughly maintained and sparse.
Dogs	Yes—on leashes only
Bikes	Yes—this park is very bike-friendly
Family-friendly	This park is a good option for families
Nearby restaurants	Restaurants and cafes are clustered around Gage St. and Green Bay Rd.

Braeside: Chicago Botanic Garden

Opened to the public in 1972, the Chicago Botanic Garden is a living museum made up of nine islands within the Forest Preserves of Cook County. Here visitors find twenty-seven display gardens and four natural areas featuring woods, prairies, rivers, shores, and lakes.

The garden's buildings and landscapes were all designed by famed architects from across the globe between 1976 and 2009. The Daniel F. and Ada L. Rice Plant Conservation Science Center, located at the south end of the garden, opened in 2009. Visitors here will can learn about the plants in the park, the native landscape of the area and about conservation efforts to protect the rare plants here.

Home gardeners will want to come and see firsthand the garden's efforts to incorporate every scrap of food and paper, composting as much as they can. The garden has committed to minimal use of fertilizers and pesticides, and staff will be happy to teach you everything they know.

All the display gardens here are uniquely engaging. A few notable ones include:

- Evening Island: a five-acre island accessed by two footbridges. Its landscape includes meadows, woods, and hills with lakes on all sides. It's a little different every day of the year, but especially great for summer sunsets.

- The Buehler Enabling Garden: a teaching garden for people of all abilities. Here you'll find raised beds and container gardens that highlight gardening techniques for people who use wheelchairs. Visitors will also find shooting fountains, waterfalls cascading in sheets, vertical gardens, and sensory plants.

- The Heritage Garden: a garden modeled after a traditional European garden divided into four quadrants, with plants from around the globe. Visit in the summer for waterlilies, lotus, and a classic physic garden full of medicinal plants.

- Dwarf Conifer Garden: especially in the winter, which can be endless and gloomy in Chicago, this place is fragrant and green. Mostly full of evergreens, it was designed as a four-season garden that plays with shapes and textures.

Stop by the visitors' center to pick up a walking map. This map includes suggested routes and points of interest, while helping visitors to understand the plants they're looking at and the landscape before them. The Prairie Views walk, and Zen Walk are two worth checking out.

Ready to sit down, but not ready to go home? The tram offers a tour of the most popular areas in the garden, with an informative narration by a guide explaining the landscape. Tours run from late April through October and take about thirty-five minutes. Purchase a ticket in the visitors' center, reservations are not necessary.

Pro tip: This place was always intended to be a space where people could interact with the gardens, and it is endlessly Instagrammable, if that's your thing. Check out #ChicagoBotanicGarden any day of the year and you'll see beautiful lights, stunning backdrops, and probably at least one post where #SheSaidYes. If you do plan to visit and hold a mini-photo shoot, just be courteous to the other visitors and try to stay out of their way. Also, stay on the trail—but that's a good rule for everyone.

Park name	Chicago Botanic Garden
Train station	Braeside
Train line	Metra: Union Pacific North
Schedule	Monday–Friday: departs from Chicago as early as 5:42 a.m., departs Braeside as late as 12:34 a.m. Saturday: departs from Chicago as early as 6:35 a.m. departs Braeside as late as 11:09 p.m. Sunday: departs from Chicago as early as 10:35 a.m. and departs Braeside as late as 10:39 p.m.
Departs from	Ogilvie Transportation Center
Round-trip travel costs	$13.50 full fare, $6.75 reduced
Entrance	From the Braeside Metra station head west on County Line Rd. for about three-quarters of a mile. There is a nice, protected footpath through Turnbull and Mary Mix McDonald Woods that follows the road.
Hours	The hours for the Chicago Botanic Garden vary seasonally. Check www.chicagobotanic.org for up-to-date information.
Distance from station to trailhead	Less than 1 mile
Miles of trails	About 4
How many acres?	385
Difficulty	★
In-park recreation options	Walking, photography, biking, birding
Amenities	Restaurants, restrooms, shopping, concessions
Safety concerns	This garden is very well kept, stay on the trails and watch your step and you should be fine.

Plants	Check out www.chicagobotanic.org/inbloom to see what's on display.
Accessibility	Wheelchairs are available for free at the information desk in the visitors' center. Accessible parking is in lots 1 and 3. Nearly all the areas of the garden are accessible, including the tram tours. Electronic convenience vehicles are available on a first-come first-served basis, for a small fee. Contact the visitors' center for more information. There are several accessible restrooms throughout the gardens.
Admission	Cars pay a $25 fee and people enter the garden for free, but you didn't bring a car today, did you?
Dogs	No, sorry
Bikes	Bikes are not allowed within the Chicago Botanic Garden, however there are ample bike racks. Additionally, a bike path surrounding the exterior of the garden is a lovely place to ride.
Family-friendly	This is a comfortable, easy hike for everyone. Stroller families will have plenty to do, it's a great place to take your aunt who doesn't move so quickly anymore, or your posh cousin coming to visit from out of town. Everyone will find something to like here.
Nearby restaurants	There are several restaurants, cafes, and even a few bars located inside the garden itself.

Fort Sheridan: Fort Sheridan Nature Preserve

Entering Fort Sheridan from the adjacent Metra station is super easy, which makes this one a good option for a quick trip. The path to and from the Metra goes through the town of Fort Sheridan and is lined with sculptures that accentuate the natural character of the area. When you enter the park, you will face an open prairie field overlooking Lake Michigan. Winds can get high here, especially when the weather is rough, so keep that in mind when planning your visit.

Starting around 1877, the Commercial Club of Chicago became concerned with labor unrest and donated 632 acres of land to the federal government to build a military garrison. After the Haymarket Riot of 1886 resulted in seven workers being killed by police after striking in support of an eight-hour workday, what became Fort Sheridan was stocked with soldiers. Frankly, they had very little to do in this scenic place until 1894, when they were used to quell labor unrest during the Pullman Strike.

Landscape designer O.C. Simonds designed the surrounding landscape for the army base in 1889. He considered military needs with the rolling terrain and ecologically sensitive bluffs and ravines. He wisely chose to make views of Lake Michigan a priority.

The military base closed for good in 1993, and today the site is a beautiful park with something for everyone. It's the only place in Lake County with free public access to Lake Michigan and it has an overlook at the top of a seventy-foot-high bluffs that is not to be missed.

Much of the landscape surrounding the fort is as pristine as it was when French explorers landed here. Today it offers unrivaled opportunities for birdwatching and recreation. The landscape of this 250-acre space is uniquely varied, with a savannah, ravines, oak forests, and at least 236 species of birds.

Many trails feature outdoor educational exhibits that tell the story of the military and natural histories of this place. The Fort Sheridan Cemetery has graves dating back to 1890 and is still actively maintained by the Army. The natural character of this place is well maintained, and it is home to plants and birds that aren't found anywhere else in the region.

Park name	Fort Sheridan Nature Preserve
Train station	Fort Sheridan
Train line	Metra: Union Pacific North
Schedule	Monday–Friday: departs Chicago as early as 5:42 a.m. and departs Fort Sheridan as late as 12:23 a.m. Saturday: departs Chicago as early as 6:35 a.m. and departs Fort Sheridan as late as 10:58 p.m. Sunday: departs Chicago as early as 10:35 a.m. and departs Fort Sheridan as late as 10:28 p.m.
Departs from	Ogilvie Transportation Center
Round-trip travel costs	$14.50 full fare, $7.25 reduced
Entrance	From the Fort Sheridan Metra station head northwest on Western Ave. and turn right onto Old Elm Rd. Take another right onto Sheridan Rd. and the entrance to the park will be across the street.
Hours	6:30 a.m. to sunset
Distance from station to trailhead	Less than .25 miles
Miles of trails	About 5
Acres	250

Difficulty	★★★
In-park recreation options	Biking, fishing, hiking, self-guided trails and exhibits, cross-country skiing
Amenities	Toilets, benches
Safety concerns	These parks have a healthy tick population. Ticks are small woodland insects that carry diseases and see mammals (that includes us) as a tasty host. Keep ticks from bothering you by wearing long pants and sleeves and cover your head with a hat or bandana.
Water	Fun fact: this is the only spot in Lake County where you can access Lake Michigan for free.
Accessibility	The trails are between 8'-14' wide and paved with crushed gravel, but there can be steep changes in elevation near the lake and bluffs.
Dogs	Yes—on leashes only
Bikes	Yes—this park is bike friendly
Nearby restaurants	Exit the park the way that you came in and you'll find no shortage of restaurants, bakeries, pizzerias, and cafes along Sheridan Rd. outside the train station.

Zion: Illinois Beach State Park and Campground

I love this hike because it's super easy to get to and if you intend to camp, it's enough of a hike from the train to your campsite to make you feel like you earned it. This is a great one for beginner backpackers, who want an easy outing close to home, or big adventure backpackers who just want to get outside for a long weekend. Illinois Beach State Park stretches along six and a half miles of the sandy shores of Lake Michigan, up to the Wisconsin border. This is the only remaining beach ridge shoreline left in Illinois, and it's home to huge amounts of plants and wildlife. It's not uncommon to spot white-tailed deer in this park. The landscape is a mix of oak savannahs, marshes, and dunes leading directly to Lake Michigan.

This park has a complex geological structure that was apparent to the first Europeans who came through the area in the 1700s. Lake Michigan's dunes contrast against the unique flora found here, creating a beach with nothing else like it in Illinois. Before European contact this place was home to Potawatomi, Chippewa, and Ottawa tribes, and the Miami before that. French explorers first arrived in the late 1600s, and by the time Illinois was a state in 1818 the area was full of hunters and trappers. In 1836 the local American Indians made a treaty with the Europeans who were moving in. The result of this treaty was that the American Indians moved westward, and the park site became part of Lake County.

Efforts to preserve the natural beauty of the area began as early as 1888, when Jens Jensen (who designed the Garfield Park Conservatory) suggested making it a regional park. The Industrial Revolution had begun, and industry was creeping in on all sides of the Great Lakes. By the 1920s, legislative efforts to preserve the natural beauty of the beach really began.

In 1948, the state bought the first land that would become Illinois Beach State Park, and in 1950, the Illinois

Dunes Preservation Society was established to protect the natural landscape here. Today, protected lands extend up to the Wisconsin border.

Once you've arrived, explore the seven miles of trails available in this park and on the northern end. There is a camp store outside the park office, several ponds for fishing, access to the Dead River, and stunning views of Lake Michigan. If the weather is warm, plan for a beach day. There is a shower facility available to campers and a visitors' center provides interpretive information about the wildlife in the park.

The park landscape includes beautiful oak woodlands, marshes, wetlands, beaches, and dunes. It's unrivaled for its beauty and environmental diversity. Walking the trails here and seeing the life teeming in the sandy wetlands makes you feel a little bit proud to know Illinois was smart enough to move to preserve this place long ago.

Camping: When you enter the park, take a left heading east towards the lake. Follow the path around south (Lake Michigan will be on your left) until you come to the park office. Check in here for your campsite. The park has 241 campgrounds available from April 1 through December 30. Reservations are only accepted from May 1 to September 30, but are recommended for holidays and weekends. There are about fifty walk-up campsites that do fill up during the summer months.

If you want to hear Lake Michigan from your sleeping bag, try campsites 302-390, but be aware that the sites can flood if the weather has been very wet, or the lake is high. If you're looking for something quieter, look at sites 104-149, which are a little further back from the lake itself. All the sites come equipped with an electrical hookup, presumably for your RV, but try not to let that bother you. All sites allow dogs and have a maximum occupancy of four people. Alcohol is not allowed. Each site comes equipped with a fire ring and picnic table. Sites 300, 392, 244, 245, 246, and 247 are all wheelchair accessible.

Reservations can be made in advance on www.reserveamerica.com, but the park recommends campers get here early if they don't have a reservation because the park is very popular on summer weekends. After you check in, the campground will be slightly north of where you are. The total distance from the Metra station in Zion to your campsite here, including the visit to the park office, should be around three miles.

Finer accommodations: Want to spend the evening enjoying the sound of Lake Michigan's waves crashing on the shore, but not into the whole sleeping in a tent thing? This is only beach in Illinois where you can stay in a hotel with beach access. The Illinois Beach Hotel, now run by Best Western, has modern accommodations, delicious food, an expansive lobby with floor-to-ceiling windows, and—yes—you can step right out of your room and onto the beach.

Park name	Adeline Jay Geo-Karis Illinois Beach State Park
Train station	Zion
Train line	Metra: Union Pacific North
Schedule	Monday–Friday: trains arrive by 8:03 a.m. and leave by 11:56 p.m. Saturday: they arrive by 8:03 a.m. and depart by 10:30 p.m. Sunday and holidays: they arrive by 7:02 a.m. and leave by 7:02 p.m.
Departs from	Ogilvie Transportation Center
Round-trip travel costs	$18 round trip full fare, $9 round trip reduced fare
Entrance	From the Zion station walk east on Shiloh Boulevard for one block, then turn right and head south on Deborah Ave. until it meets at a dead end with 29th St. There is an entrance to the park here.
Hours	Sunrise to sunset

Distance from station to trailhead	About .5 miles
Miles of trails	About 7
Acrea	4,160 in Illinois Beach State Park
Difficulty	★★★
Finer accommodations	Illinois Beach Hotel: the only hotel in Illinois located directly on the beach
In-park recreation options	Biking, camping, fishing, hiking, swimming, concessions, hiking, cross country-skiing, geocaching, SCUBA diving
Amenities	Camp store, firewood, picnic tables, concession stands, changing rooms, and a marina. The campground includes access to showers.
Safety concerns	Lake Michigan can be a hazard when weather is bad, or water and wind are high. Keep clear of the water if these conditions exist.
Plants	Over 650 species of plants have been found just in the dunes area alone. Visit the dry areas in the warm weather and you might spot prickly pear cactus. Wildflowers are abundant during the spring. Marshes support cattails, big bluestem, grasses, and sedges.
Water	This place is a popular swimming beach in the summer months.
Geology	Notable bluffs, dunes, and sandy beaches
Accessibility	Six accessible sites are present in the campground near the accessible restrooms. Illinois Beach Hotel is also accessible. There is an accessible fishing pier.
Dogs	Yes—on leashes only
Bikes	Yes—this park is bike friendly
Nearby restaurants	There is no shortage of cafes, bars, and restaurants around Sherman Road.

MILWAUKEE DISTRICT NORTH

Forest Glen and Edgebrook: LaBagh Woods and the North Branch Trail

This one is entirely within Chicago city limits, so it's ideal for getting into the woods when you're short on time. Once you enter the park, you have access to the North Branch Trail System, which can carry you as far as Glencoe and the Skokie Lagoons. *Pro tip: It might be fun for an adventurous biker to ride this path all the way north and catch the UP-North Metra home at Braeside.*

Exit the Metra station toward Forest Glen Ave. and turn left. Here, Forest Glen community gardeners have done a beautiful job of landscaping the area and they should be commended. Continue past that and you will come to a wide-open field. This is the entrance point for Forest Glen Woods. Hikers will want to take the path straight ahead when they enter the park. In about half a block, you will be able to cross over to the other side of Forest Glen Ave., which puts you in LaBagh Woods. Follow the path southeast towards Gompers Park if you're interested in seeing the beginning of the North Branch Trail System.

There are plenty of deer and game trails here that can be easily mistaken for paths extending out from the big, wide, paved bike trail that runs throughout this branch of the system. Be careful if you are on one of these, it might be a game trail and you might encounter a deer at rest. If you do, keep your distance and back away.

LaBagh Woods is a beautiful example of woodlands with some significant tree cover of huge old oaks, maples, and cottonwoods. Visit during the summer or when flooding is high, and it can feel downright swampy. During the growing season visitors will find wild geranium, Indian plantain, turtlehead, blue flag iris, marsh blazing star, and hop sedge. Visit during the spring and fall migration season and this place is alive with birds. The Sauganash Prairie Grove in particular, near the northwest side of this site, can get cacophonous with birdsong. Keep an eye out for spring warblers, tanagers, and sparrows. During the winter months you'll spot the big nests for Cooper's and red-tailed hawks high in the treetops. Mink and other water-loving mammals can be spotted along the riverbanks.

Here, you can turn around and head back the way you came to explore the rest of the trail or you can continue to follow the path until it comes to Pulaski Rd. Take a left and the entrance to Bohemian National Cemetery will be on your left. This still-active cemetery has an abundance of unique headstones and grave markers, and is known for its rare glass-fronted columbariums. There are two; an older one dating back to the cemetery's founding in the late nineteenth century, and a more modern one designed to mimic the brick walls found outside Wrigley Field. (It's even got some genuine Wrigley bleachers donated by the Cubs when they renovated the park.) Exit the cemetery at Kildare Ave., take a left onto W. Bryn Mawr Ave., and you'll be able to re-enter LaBagh Woods at an entrance about one block west of N. Kenneth Ave. You will now be on the north side of the Chicago River.

If instead of heading south towards LaBagh Woods you headed north towards Thaddeus S. "Ted" Lechowicz Woods, you would see a lot of similar landscape. In the winter, after a big snowstorm, come here to check out the sledding hill and slide freely down the slope.

Continue following the path to the left and head north, as far as you like. The path will take you over and across the river several times. There is a somewhat steep footbridge over train tracks that can be quite a vertical climb and it makes a good place to turn around if you're just out for a short hike. Alternately, continue north just a little further and exit on the north side of Central Ave. Here, you can catch up with the Milwaukee District North Line Metra at the Edgebrook station.

Park name	LaBagh Woods
Train Station	Forest Glen
Train line	Metra: Milwaukee District North
Schedule	Monday–Friday: departs downtown as early as 6:25 a.m. and departs Forest Glen as late as 11:39 p.m. Saturday: departs downtown as early as 8:25 a.m. and departs Forest Glen as late as 11:31 p.m. Sunday: departs downtown as early as 8:35 a.m. and departs Forest Glen as late as 11:31 p.m.
Departs from:	Union Station
Round-trip travel costs	$11 full fare, $5.50 reduced
Entrance	From the Forest Glen Metra station head north towards North Forest Glen Ave. Take a right and follow it towards Forest Glen Woods; the entrance will be on your left.
Hours	Sunrise to sunset
Distance from station to trailhead	Less than .25 miles
Miles of trails	Forest Glen Woods links up with the North Branch Trail System, which offers 20 miles of paved and unpaved trails
Acres	160 in LaBagh Woods alone
Difficulty	★★
In-park recreation options	Bicycling, hiking, cross-country skiing, picnicking
Amenities	Picnic shelters Portable restrooms
Safety concerns	Seasonal flooding, especially at the underpasses, can get quite high.

Plants	Woodlands, wetlands, marshes, swaps, prairies, fields
Water	The Chicago River runs throughout this trail system.
Family-friendly	This is suitable for families, but it is also popular with bikers so please stick to the right and let faster traffic pass on the left.
Accessibility	The paths are wide, largely flat, and paved with crushed gravel.
Dogs	Yes—on leashes only
Bikes	Yes—this park is bike friendly
Nearby restaurants	There are no shortage of restaurants, breweries, and cafes around the intersection of Central Ave. and Devon Ave. If you head towards the western end of the forest preserves and Devon, however, you'll find the legendary Superdawg Drive-In.

Morton Grove: Frank Bobrytzke Forest and the North Branch Trail

A great option for day hikers looking to get in a fair amount of mileage. The five-minute walk from the train station to the park goes through an adorable little suburb. Enter the park at Frank Bobrytzke Forest and follow the trail to the left. You'll wander through Miami Woods. Cross over the river at Oakton St. and head back north on the opposite side of the river.

Cross to the north side of the road at Dempster St.and continue north on the path. If you're interested in checking out the Morton Grove Historical Museum, continue east on Dempster for one block and take a left at Lake St. The museum will be on the south end of Harrier Park. Exit the museum and walk north through Harrier Park and you'll be able to rejoin the North Branch Trail at Linne Woods. Follow the path ahead, crossing over the woods, and you'll be able to access several notable loops.

Visit Miami Woods during the springtime and see a carpet of wildflowers among the restored prairie. Beginning in the 1970s, volunteers worked to restore this once-neglected piece of prairie. Today visitors will frequently find bluffs with bur, white, and Hill's oak, and abundant sparrows, yellowthroats, eastern kingbirds, and warblers. Today visitors to Linne Woods will find a dense canopy of oaks and hickories, with black cherry and ironwood understories.

Head north and cross back over the river at Beckwith Rd. and check out the trails on the eastern end of the park. Follow the trails heading south back towards Dempster Rd. Follow Lincoln Ave. south until it becomes Lehigh Ave., which will lead you back towards the train station.

Park name	Frank Bobrytzke Forest and the North Branch Trail
Train station	Morton Grove
Train line	Metra: Milwaukee District North
Schedule	Monday–Friday: departs Chicago as early as 6:25 A.M. and departs Morton Grove as late as 11:31 p.m. Saturday: departs Chicago as early as 8:35 a.m. and departs Morton Grove around 11:23 p.m. Sunday: departs Chicago as early as 8:35 a.m. and departs Morton Grove as late as 11:23 p.m.
Departs from	Union Station
Round-trip travel costs	$11 full fare, $5.50 reduced
Entrance	From the Morton Grove Metra station head northwest towards Lehigh Ave., take a right at Lincoln Ave. and the park will be directly ahead of you.
Hours	Sunrise to sunset
Distance from station to trailhead	Less than .5 miles
Miles of trails	About 7, with access to the 36.7-mile-long North Branch Trail
Acres	About 500 in Frank Bobrytzke Forest and Linne Woods
Difficulty	★★
In-park recreation options	Hiking, bicycling, walking, cross-country skiing
Amenities	Picnic shelters, portable bathrooms
Safety concerns	Ticks can be a concern year round. Flooding can be a concern if the weather has been wet.

Plants	This trail travels through oak and hickory forests.
Water	This trail runs alongside the North Branch of the Chicago River
Accessibility	The trail is wide, flat, and often paved. There are some changes in elevation.
Dogs	Yes—on leashes only
Bikes	Yes—this park is very bike friendly
Family-friendly	This one is near to the train station and has a lot of trails, so this is a good option for families.
Nearby restaurants	There are a fair number of restaurants along Dempster Ave., and a few along Lincoln Ave. adjacent to the train station.

Northbrook:
Somme Preserves

This trio of nature preserves includes Somme Prairie, Somme Prairie Grove, and Somme Woods, and is home to an astonishing abundance of prairie plants, flowers, and grasses—all less than ninety minutes from downtown Chicago. If you like hikes on narrow, rustic, and roughly maintained trails, put Somme Preserves on your list.

Enter the preserves through the Somme Woods Picnic Grove. The Forest Preserves of Cook County manages these parks, but trails do not show up on the official maps. That's because for FPCC to consider them trails they would need to be wider, with more frequent mowing or paving. Instead, the trails in this park are maintained by local stewards who leave them intentionally rough so visitors can feel very immersed in nature. Hikers can only walk single file, so visit during the summer to feel what it's like to have prairie grasses closing in on all sides of you. The stewards made that choice intentionally by planting rush (*Juncus tenuis*), a grassy plant that can grow even when people and animals trample on them. This not only protects the landscape, but it makes the trails a bit easier to find among the tallgrasses.

If you enter from Waukegan and Dundee roads you will enter at Somme Woods, the easternmost of the three parks. Here, visitors will find seventy acres of restored habitat that is still under active restoration. On over half of the 150 acres found here, invasive plants are rare, and wildflowers and songbirds are abundant. Rare prairie plants include leadplant, cream false indigo, prairie brome, prairie gentian, hoary puccoon, and dropseed grass. On the rest, volunteers and stewards are actively working to remove invasive plants, non-native trees, brush, and buckthorn, and allow the natural woodlands, wetlands, savannas, and prairies the chance to restore themselves. This is a beautiful example of where the oak woodlands meet the prairie. In some parts of these woods the grassy undergrowth practically dances due to the sheer number of birds that can be found here year round.

When you've hiked your heart's content in Somme Woods, head for the intersection of Dundee Rd. and Waukegan again. There is a small trail leading to that intersection from the western edge of the parking lot within Somme Woods, which I recommend over walking along Dundee Rd. There is no crosswalk at Dundee and Waukegan roads, so please use caution. The entrance to Somme Prairie Grove is on the western side of Waukegan Rd.

Inside Somme Prairie Grove, visitors will find a rare savanna ecosystem. The towering bur oaks create a habitat for wildlife not normally found in this region. Visitors here will spy orchard orioles, eastern kingbirds, savannah blazing stars, as well as rare butterflies and dragonflies. More than 400 rare or uncommon plants and animals call this place home. Volunteers have worked diligently since the 1980s to restore this rare tallgrass savanna. Today, its eighty-five acres are considered one of the finest examples of an ecosystem brought back to life from the brink of destruction.

The westernmost of the three parks is Somme Prairie Nature Preserve, which is still undergoing restoration. A small hiking trail has recently been created within this park, but it is not easy to access from Somme Prairie Grove. If you wish to explore it, cross to the southern side of Dundee Rd. and use the sidewalk to access the trail from just behind the post office.

These three parks are impressive examples of how the hard work of a dedicated group of volunteers can protect and restore our natural landscape. Visit www. sommepreserve.org to learn more about the plants, animals in this park, and the conservation efforts that have created this habitat. You'll also find trail maps and season-specific, self-guided tour information through that organization. Trail maps may be available in a box at the trailhead, and if they are, they often come with seasonally themed poems to contemplate during your hike, which is an amenity you won't find anywhere else.

Park name	Somme Prairie Nature Preserve, Somme Prairie, Somme Woods
Train station	Northbrook
Train line	Metra: Milwaukee District North
Schedule	Monday–Friday: departs Chicago as early as 6:25 a.m. Departs Northbrook as late as 11:17 p.m. Saturday: departs Chicago as early as 8:35 a.m. and departs Northbrook as late as 11:10 p.m. Sunday: departs Chicago as early as 8:35 a.m. and departs Northbrook as late as 11:10 p.m.
Departs from	Union Station
Round-trip travel costs	$13.50 full fare, $6.75 reduced
Entrance	From the Northbrook Metra station head right onto Shermer Rd., follow that until it comes to Waukegan Rd. and take a left. Take another left onto Dundee Rd. and Somme Woods will be ahead of you. There is no crosswalk at the corner of Dundee Rd. and Waukegan Rd. so please use caution.
Hours	Sunrise to sunset
Distance from station to trailhead	About 1.25 miles
Miles of trails	More than 5
Acres	433
Difficulty	★★★

In-park recreation options	Hiking, walking, birding, biking, picnicking
Amenities	Picnic shelter, portable toilets, maps and poems at the trailheads
Safety concerns	The trails are roughly maintained, and the natural fall of debris can create a tripping hazard.
Water	The North Branch of the Chicago River flows through Somme Woods, but lakes, lagoons, pools, and creeks can be found throughout all three parks.
Geology	Somme Prairie Grove sits on top of a moraine, which means glacial erratics can be found throughout the park. Wherever you see a granite boulder that looks out of place, it was likely left there by a melting glacier about 10,000 years ago.
Accessibility	The trails are roughly maintained and narrow. They can be flooded during wet months. In many places the trail is made of logs on top of some of the muddier parts. If leaves have fallen, the trail can be difficult to see.
Dogs	Yes—on leashes only
Bikes	Not allowed, sorry
Family-friendly	This one is a little further from the train station, and entering the park involves crossing a four-lane road without a crosswalk, so it may not be a good option for families with small children.
Nearby restaurants	There are a handful of restaurants and cafes on Shermer Rd.

Libertyville–Prairie Crossing: Des Plaines River Trail, Old School Forest Preserve

This is the northernmost spot on the Des Plaines River Trail that you can get to on the train. Weekend warriors committed to completing the entire trail will want to use this spot to start the not-quite eighteen mile trek north through mostly connected paths and forests to the Wisconsin border. Pick me up some of those squeaky cheese curds while you're up there, will ya?

When you enter the Des Plaines River Trail from Oak Spring Road you will be in Wilmot Woods. Take the path south past Riverside Park and you can enter Old School Forest Preserve south of Saint Mary's Rd. Here, interconnecting paths loop all over the 540-acre preserve.

Here, you'll find a popular trail for hiking, walking, birding, and cross-country skiing. This has one of the area's best sledding hills, so consider that for winter outings. Old School Nature Preserve is named in honor of the now-closed Bradley School, which stood near the southeast corner of the park and was founded as a log cabin in 1873.

Turn around and head back north the way that you came. Continue north when you cross Oak Spring Rd. and you'll enter Minear Park, which includes stunning views of Lake Minear. Adler Park directly north of Minear is a lovely community park, with a picnic area, frisbee golf, and a flower garden. In the winter this is a popular spot for ice skating, cross-country skiing, and sledding. You'll also find a restroom, concessions, and a warming shelter.

Continue further north and you'll come to Independence Grove Forest Preserve. The Independence

Grove Forest Preserve visitors' center is open daily from 9 a.m.–4:30 p.m. and includes nature and history exhibits, photo displays, and art galleries. The panoramic windows overlooking the lake and preserve are a beautiful place to warm yourself after a chilly winter hike. A café is open seasonally.

Independence Grove Nature Preserve includes 1,151 acres and over six miles of trails. Visitors here will find a 115-acre lake surrounded by prairies and woodlands. You can rent fishing boats, canoes, kayaks, stand up paddleboards, and pedal boats at the marina from spring through fall, as well as bikes, quadracycles, and adaptive trikes. You can also pick up bait, tackle, fishing licenses, and snacks.

During the warm months, check out the 400-foot-long sandy swimming beach along the south bay of the lake. There is a beach house with washrooms, showers, and lockers. Beach passes are available at the visitors' center. Daily beach admission is free for kids ages two and under, $4 for Lake County residents, and $7 for nonresidents.

Previously this land was an abandoned quarry. When Lake County took possession of it in 1978 the dream was that the quarry could be reclaimed for recreational and natural use. Today, birds stop here on their migration as far north as the Arctic circle.

Park name	Old School Forest Preserve
Train station	Libertyville–Prairie Crossing
Train line	Metra: Milwaukee District North
Schedule	Monday–Friday: departs Chicago as early as 6:25 a.m. and departs Libertyville as late as 10:55 p.m. Saturday: departs Chicago as early as 8:35 a.m. and departs Libertyville as late as 10:48 p.m. Sunday: departs Chicago as early as 8:35 a.m. and departs Libertyville as late as 10:48 p.m.
Departs from	Union Station
Round-trip travel costs	$16.50 full fare, $8.25 reduced
Entrance	From the Libertyville Metra station head southwest and turn right towards Lake St. Take a left onto Lake St. and another left onto Milwaukee Ave. Take another right onto Appley Ave. and follow that until you see Oak Spring Rd. Take a left and the Des Plaines River Trail will be ahead of you on the left.
Hours	Sunrise to sunset
Distance from station to trailhead	About 1 mile
Miles of trails	The Des Plaines River Trail has about 30 miles of continuous trail.
Acres	The Des Plaines River Trail includes about 13,000 acres of vegetation, wetlands, and paths.
Difficulty	★★
In-park recreation options:	Hiking, biking, fishing, canoeing, sledding
Amenities	Toilets

Safety concerns	The Des Plaines River Trail currently breaks near Allison Woods where Milwaukee Ave. crosses through the preserves just south of Willow Rd. Hikers should carefully cross Milwaukee Ave. using the designated walkway at Winkelman Rd., then following Winkleman Rd. until it rejoins the Des Plaines River Trail. Seasonal flooding is common in the sections of the path between Touhy and North avenues. Depending on the weather and conditions parts of the trail, particularly underpasses, may have standing water.
Plants	Large old oaks dominate these woodlands, which contrast with the small prairies that make up the landscape.
Water	This trail runs alongside the Des Plaines River, which means that flooding can be a concern.
Accessibility	The trail is stone, generally flat and does not include any stairs or steep elements. However, it can have roots or debris, that can leave it with less than the standard 10' width. There is a bridge over Lake Cook Rd that connects to the forest preserve.
Dogs	Yes—on leashes only
Bikes	Yes—this park is bike friendly
Family-friendly	This one is a little further from the trailhead, but the variety of options within the park are good options for families with kids.
Nearby restaurants	Libertyville has no shortage of gastropubs, bars, cafes, restaurants, and diners located primarily along Milwaukee Ave. around the train station.

Round Lake:
Hart's Wood Park

Hart's Woods is an adorable little community park, that's extremely family oriented. Within this park you'll find playgrounds, soccer fields, as well as hiking trails. This place is also home to the recently renovated Prairie Grass Nature Museum, which has interpretive and informative programming for children of all ages, but adults might find something they enjoy as well. Say hello to Butterscotch, the king corn snake.

One building west of the Prairie Grass Nature Museum, visitors will find the Children's Neighborhood Museum, a tot-sized neighborhood built to the height of small kiddos. Children ages one to six are invited to play here and try on different roles within a community.

The rest of Hart's Woods packs a surprising amount into its small acreage. Hart's Hill is a popular sledding hill in the wintertime. A stand of bur oaks generally keeps their leaves most of the winter, so it's a place to find some color in the colder months. An outdoor challenge course is suitable for school-age kids, or adults looking to develop teambuilding skills. It is recommended for groups of ten or more and popular with scouting troops, school and church groups, and community organizations.

Overall Hart's Woods is a fantastic option for families with kids of any age.

Bonus hike: Not too tired after seeing Hart's Woods? Take the half-mile path to the entrance to Nippersink Forest Preserve and check out the observation points to see Round Lake Marsh North. Bring binoculars, this is a popular spot for birders.

Directions: Exit the park by turning right onto Hart Rd., take a left and follow Haywood Dr. until you come to Nippersink Rd. The entrance to the park will be directly ahead of you.

Park name	Hart's Woods Park
Train station	Round Lake
Train line	Metra: Milwaukee District North
Schedule	Monday–Friday: arrives in Round Lake at 8:24 a.m., leaves by 10:32 p.m. Saturday: departs from Chicago around 8:35 p.m., leaves Round Lake by 10:34 p.m. Sunday: departs from Chicago around 8:35 a.m., departs from Round Lake at 10:25 p.m.
Departs from	Union Station
Round-trip travel costs	$18, $9 reduced fare
Entrance	Exit the Round Lake Metra stop, and turn towards Railroad Ave. Turn right on Railroad Ave. until you take a slight left onto Hart Rd. The park will be ahead of you on the right.
Hours	Sunrise to sunset
Distance from station to trailhead	About .5 miles, with sidewalks on both sides of the street
Miles of trails	About 1.5
Acres	33
Difficulty	★★
In-park recreation options	Bike racks, grill, lagoon/lake, natural area, open space, parking, picnic shelter, playground, restrooms, skate park, soccer
Amenities	Prairie Grass Nature Museum Children's Neighborhood Museum
Safety concerns	The trails in the wooded area here can become obscured during the fall and winter months, step cautiously because the ground beneath can be uneven.

Plants	Small stands of oak woodland create opportunities for easy hikes for small kids.
Water	There is an aquatics center on site.
Accessibility	The trails are between 8' and 14' wide and paved in crushed gravel, which is considered accessible. Other trails are mowed, and the surface is considered less accessible.
Dogs	Yes—on leashes only
Bikes	This park is bike friendly
Admission	Prairie Grass Nature Museum (free) Children's Neighborhood Museum ($6 daily fee, per child, max 30 children per day, first-come, first-served)
Family-friendly	This is a very family friendly option, especially for families with small kiddos.
Nearby restaurants	There are plenty of cafes, bars, and restaurants in the area surrounding the Round Lake Metra Station.

Round Lake: Nippersink Forest Preserve

Enter Nippersink Forest Preserve from the recently added entrance on Nippersink Ave. There's no place for cars to park here, but that's not a problem for you today. This .75-mile path has observation points overlooking rich marshes. In the summertime the area sings with wildlife and activity from birds and fish. In the wintertime, it's a frosty sea of blue against the golden landscape of the surrounding prairie.

Nippersink Forest Preserve is an excellent example of one of our rarest natural communities. Here you'll find rare species of plants, and high-quality natural areas that require protection. Endangered birds and plants have been spotted here. This park is tucked into several residential neighborhoods, so the path is a little more heavily trafficked.

Nippersink is also home to stunning examples of wetlands and emergent marshes. On the lower parts of the park, you'll find open ponds, on the higher end towering oak hickory woodlands provide habitat for native and migrating birds. A portion of Squaw Creek flows through this property. During the summer months, especially if the rain has been high, this can be a powerful flow of water. In the wintertime it's a graceful trickle with icy accents. Either way, it's best viewed from on top of the bridge.

In terms of parks, Nippersink is a new one. It only began to be acquired by the county in 2002. The two lakes total thirteen acres and were man-made in 1965. It's common to find geese and other migrating birds taking refuge on them. During the warmer months, when things get marshy, great blue herons, white herons, egrets, and red-tailed hawks find an attractive habitat here. Visit at any season to hear an abundance of birdsong.

The trail will take you all around the lakes, and you can

spend quite of bit of time traversing them all. The main entrance to the park is on the south end at Belvedere Rd., near Nippersink Lake. Around that lake, visitors will find an engaging story told through stations placed around the lake. It's designed for kids, but it's also a few miles from the trailhead where you entered. Don't forget, you must turn back and get to the train, so make sure your kiddo is comfortable with what could be considered a Big Hike before you go this far. Alternately, consider biking this one.

Park name	Nippersink Forest Preserve
Train station	Round Lake
Train line	Metra: Milwaukee District North
Schedule	Monday–Friday: arrives in Round Lake at 8:24 a.m., leaves by 10:32 p.m. Saturday: departs from Chicago around 8:35 p.m., leaves Round Lake by 10:34 p.m. Sunday: departs from Chicago around 8:35 a.m., departs from Round Lake at 10:25 p.m.
Departs from	Union Station
Round-trip travel costs	$18, $9 reduced fare
Entrance	From Round Lake Metra turn left onto North Cedar Lake Rd., then take a right onto West Nippersink Rd. for about .75 miles. The trailhead for the preserve will be on the right.
Hours	6:30 a.m. to sunset
Distance from station to trailhead	About 1 mile, with sidewalks along the entirety of the path.
Miles of trails	3

Acres	329
Difficulty	★★
In-park recreation options	Fishing (catch and release) is very popular here. Also hiking, biking, birding, picnicking, cross-country skiing, summer camps
Amenities	Clean vault toilets, fishing pier, picnic shelters
Safety concerns	Trails can become mushy following heavy rains.
Plants	Much of this preserve is a mix of prairies and marshes. Trails are built onto high ground and offer beautiful views of the lakes.
Water	Marshes and lakes
Accessibility	The paths here are wide and flat, with gently rolling terrain. Paved with crushed gravel, they can get mushy when it's wet out.
Dogs	Yes—on leashes only
Bikes	Yes—this park is bike friendly
Family-friendly	Very. This is a great option for kiddos and, especially families on bikes.
Nearby restaurants	There are plenty of cafes, bars, and restaurants in the area surrounding the Round Lake Metra station.

Ingleside: Grant Woods Forest Preserve

This is a stunningly beautiful park that's super easy to get to from the Metra station. Directly in front of the station is the Chain-O-Lakes bike path, which runs from Fox Lake on the western end all the way to Grant Woods North. Step onto the bike path, take a right from the train station and you'll walk directly into Grant Woods Forest Preserve.

Visitors will enter from the Rollins Rd. side of the park and cross over enter the park. Entering from the southern end puts you inside a towering oak forest that runs directly alongside a vast expanse of prairie that was never farmed. Follow the trail and you'll come to an even larger interior field. Check this place out in the summertime if you want to see grasses that are taller you. Hawks and raptors love this place because the vast open fields are full of mice, voles, squirrels, and other tasty varmints.

In June 2019 Lake County went the extra mile to register some of the most pristine prairies in this park in the Illinois Nature Preserves System. This added an extra level of ecological protection to this rare example of what many of our backyards used to look like. Over 130 acres of prairie within this park has already been registered with the Illinois Nature Preserves System.

Grants Woods is home to prairies, woodlands, and marshes full of wildlife. Here visitors will find a gently rolling pristine landscape and no shortage of cattails. And check this place out if you're into tamarack bogs! Tamarack trees are conifers that can grow eighty feet tall and live up to 200 years, but this is about as far south as they can survive. They grow particularly well in bogs with plenty of sphagnum mosses. Birds are abundant on in the woodlands year round. They're easy to spot in the prairie when all the grasses are in seed, and the birds are preparing for winter.

Year-round visitors will see deer, hawks, and other wildlife. In the summer the grasses tower over everyone on the path and bluebirds call this place home; in the springtime the frogs get vocal. This place is also home to Lake County's only known stand of wild Kentucky coffee trees, which provides a glimpse into the American Indian history of the region. The low-lying marshy areas on the northeast side of Grants Woods South are so full of cattails that their fluff drifts off like snow in the breeze.

If high-mileage hikes are what you're looking for meander north and enter Grant Woods North, where you'll be able to access another three or more miles of trails. Otherwise, continue back towards the entrance along Rollins Rd. and exit the way you came.

Park name	Grant Woods Forest Preserve
Train station	Ingleside
Train line	Metra: Milwaukee District North
Schedule	Monday–Friday: From Chicago as early as 6:25 a.m., and leaving Ingleside as late as 10:26 p.m. Saturday: leaving Chicago as early as 8:35 a.m. and leaving Ingleside as late as 10:28 p.m. Sunday: Leaving Chicago as early as 8:35 a.m. and leaving Ingleside as late as 10:28 p.m.
Departs from	Union Station
Round-trip travel costs	$19 full fare, $9.25 reduced
Entrance	From the Ingleside Metra station exit and turn to the right. You'll now be on the Chain-O-Lakes bike path. This designated biking path is commonly used by walkers, but it does run alongside the road without a barrier in between, so use caution. Follow this path for about 1 mile and you will enter the Grant Woods Forest Preserve.

Hours	6:30 a.m. to sunset
Distance from station to trailhead	About 1 mile on a designated bike path that runs alongside the road
Miles of trails	More than 10
Acres	1,226
Difficulty	★★★
In-park recreation options	Biking, canoeing/kayaking, fishing, hiking, snowmobiling, summer camps, cross-country skiing
Amenities	Picnic shelter, clean vault toilet, water fountains
Safety concerns	Year-round ticks can be a concern at this park.
Plants	Prairies and woodlands, as well as wetlands
Water	Wetlands
Accessibility	The path is wide and flat. It is made of crushed gravel and can become soggy in wet weather. There are some hills but no steep grades.
Dogs	Yes—on leashes only
Bikes	Yes—this park is bike friendly
Family-friendly	The path from the train station to the park is down the side of the road, in a marked path, but without any barrier from traffic. This may not make it a good option for children.
Nearby restaurants	There are a small handful of cafes and local fast food joints around the Ingleside Metra station, but not many.

UNION PACIFIC NORTHWEST

Des Plaines: Des Plaines River Trail, Camp Ground Road Woods

This stretch of the Des Plaines River Trail includes easy access to some rougher terrain to hike on the southern end. Camp Ground Road Woods, sadly, does not have a campground but it does have shaded paths, river access, and abundant wildlife. *Pro tip: Birders have positive things to say about the number of orioles in this park.*

The trails are well maintained, wide, and a mix of either concrete pavement or crushed gravel. The deer have no natural predators and it's not uncommon to see people here hand-feeding them. Don't do this, both because a deer bite could be pretty nasty, and because it encourages dependence by the deer. Leave them to forage for food on their own. Still, nature photographers will have no challenge getting detailed up-close pictures of deer in this park. The path can be muddy during flooding, so be aware of that if rain has been heavy.

If you entered from Des Plaines, you'll be just north of Northwestern Woods. Big Bend Lake is just north of there. An adventurous hiker might want to walk the eight miles directly north to visit the River Trail Nature Center, but a bike ride might be a less exhausting way to go.

South of the entrance you'll find Algonquin Woods and Iroquois Woods, which both run alongside the Des Plaines River Trail and offer unpaved paths through towering oaks and gorgeous native landscapes.

Continue following the path north and you'll come to Kloempken Prairie, which has been beautifully restored since the 1990s. There are no trails within the prairie, but it is a beautiful example of our restored landscape and if you visit during the spring or fall, it will likely be vibrant with birds.

Park name	Camp Ground Road Woods
Train station	Des Plaines
Train line	Union Pacific Northwest
Schedule	Monday–Friday: departs Chicago as early as 5:55 a.m. and Des Plaines as late as 12:54 a.m. Saturday: departs Chicago as early as 8:30 a.m. and returns from Des Plaines as late as 10:44 p.m. Sunday and holidays: departs Chicago as early as 9:30 a.m. and returns from Des Plaines as late as 9:48 p.m.
Departs from	Ogilvie Transportation Center
Round-trip travel costs	$12.50 full fare, $6.25 reduced
Entrance	From the Des Plaines Metra stop head southeast and take a left onto Pearson Street. Take a right onto Miner Street cross the river, descend a staircase and the entrance to the Des Plaines River Trail will be directly head of you.
Hours	Sunrise to sunset
Distance from station to trailhead	About .25 miles
Miles of trails	The Des Plaines River Trail has about 30 miles of continuous trail.
Acres	The Des Plaines River Trail includes about 13,000 acres of vegetation, wetlands, and paths.
Difficulty	★★
In-park recreation options	Hiking, biking, cross-country skiing, picnicking, fishing, ice fishing (Axehead Lake)
Amenities	Picnic shelters, portable bathrooms

Safety concerns	The Des Plaines River Trail currently breaks for the Union Pacific Railroad crossing between Golf Rd. and Central Ave. Crossing is prohibited for safety reasons. The Forest Preserves of Cook County has plans to build a footbridge here, but a completion date is not set. Since you cannot safely cross the river at this level, cross via the pedestrian crosswalk at Bender and Golf roads. You will be able to rejoin the trail on the other side. There is another break in the trail near Allison Woods where Milwaukee Ave. crosses through the preserves just south of Willow Rd. Hikers should carefully cross Milwaukee Ave. using the designated walkway at Winkelman Rd., then following Winkleman Rd. until it rejoins the Des Plaines River Trail. Seasonal flooding is common in the sections of the path between Touhy and North avenues. Depending on the weather and conditions parts of the trail, particularly underpasses, may have standing water.
Water	This trail runs alongside the Des Plaines River, which means that flooding can be a concern.
Accessibility	The trail is stone, generally flat, and does not include any stairs or steep elements. However, it can have roots or debris that can leave it with less than the standard 10' width.
Dogs	Yes—on leashes only
Bikes	Yes—this park is bike friendly
Family-friendly	The distance from the train station and the accessibility of the trails makes this a good option for families.
Nearby restaurants	Most restaurants can be found along Busse Highway in between the train stations.

Palatine: Deer Grove and Camp Reinberg

This one nearly didn't make the cut in this guide because there is such a long walk from the train station to the park. It's a nearly three-mile hike down the Palatine Trail before you even get to the trailhead. The reason it was included is because if you are willing and capable of making the journey, you can spend the night at Camp Reinberg, which offers some of the only year-round camping in Cook County. It's also exactly the kind of park I was hoping to find when I set out to write this book.

Adventure seekers, weekend warriors, and backpackers will want to put this one on their list. There are over fifteen miles of trails available within the park, which is enough to explore plenty of trails over the course of a weekend, without a lot of backtracking. Including the nearly three miles to get to Camp Reinberg from the Palatine Metra, it's easy to hike twenty miles or more in a weekend.

Camp Reinberg offers year-round camping facilities for tents, RVs, and groups, as well as both large and small heated cabins. Each campsite can fit up to six people, with a fire ring and picnic table. Most campsites are a short walk away from the parking lot, which is nice as you've decided you don't need a car for this trip. The campsites are in a beautiful wooded setting with a privacy fence between the campground and nearby Quentin Rd. Tent campsites (numbers 6-18) are set further back from the road than the cabins or electric campsites, so look at those campsites if you're seeking privacy and solitude.

Large cabins fit up to ten people, and have heating, air conditioning, and ceiling fans. They offer private, accessible restrooms with a toilet and shower. They all have a porch, picnic table, and fire ring.

Small cabins fit up to eight people, and have ceiling fans as well as a porch, picnic table, and fire ring. Small cabins are not heated or air conditioned.

There is a group campsite available with space for twenty-five people.

The rolling terrain was shaped by glaciers 10,000 years ago. The result is that hikers on the western end of the preserve will find thick forests of burr, white, red, and brown oaks, accented with goldenrod and prairie grasses. In the low-lying center portions of the preserve, creeks meet to form a marshy area with abundant wildlife and year-round birdsong. If you like roughly maintained paths with some change in elevation, check out the yellow trail.

Deer Grove has fifteen and a half miles of trails, some of which can be a challenge. The eastern half of this preserve features open wetlands, fields, and both prairies and savannahs in the process of being restored. The western side has dense forests and rolling terrains. Don't be surprised if a white-tailed deer crosses your path.

There are no concessions in the park, and not much in the way of nearby restaurants. At the southeastern corner of Deer Grove East, you will find a Walgreens, and at the corner of Dundee and Quentin roads there's a Mobil gas station. Beyond that, plan to pack in and out all your provisions.

Bonus hike: The long walk from the Palatine Metra stop wasn't enough for you? Try this instead. Get off the train at the Barrington Metra station. Then head northeast and turn right onto Klingenberg Lane. Follow the sidewalk along US-14 until you come to East Hillside Rd. and turn left. Follow this path for almost one and a half miles and the access path to Deer Grove Forest Preserve will be on your right.

There are sidewalks for about the first half of this path, but the second half does not have sidewalks. There is a marked biking and walking path on the side of the road, but there is no barrier between pedestrians and traffic (marked 30 mph). Use caution.

After you enter Deer Grove Forest Preserve from East Hillside Road take the first path to the left at the fork.

Continue on the path ahead, past Deer Grove #5, around Deer Grove Pond; continue left at the next fork and cross North Quinten Rd. Camp Reinberg will be directly ahead of you. You will also have hiked about four and a half miles, and you're probably ready for a rest.

Park name	Deer Grove and Deer Grove East
Train station	Palatine
Train line	Metra: Union Pacific Northwest
Schedule	Monday–Friday: departs Chicago as early as 5:55 a.m. and departs Palatine as late as 12:35 a.m. Saturday: departs Chicago as early as 8:30 a.m. and departs Palatine as late as 10:25 p.m. Sunday and holidays: departs Chicago as early as 9:30 a.m. and departs Palatine as late as 9:25 p.m.
Departs from	Ogilvie Transportation Center
Round-trip travel costs	$15.50 full fare, $7.75 reduced fare
Entrance	From the Palatine Metra station take a right onto Wood St. and join up with the Palatine Trail. Follow the Palatine Trail until it comes to the intersection at Tom T. Hamilton Park and take a left. Continue following the Palatine trail until you come to the intersection with Dundee Rd. Take a left and cross to the northwest corner of the intersection of Dundee and Quentin roads, where you will be able to enter the park. Camp Reinberg will be about one-half mile ahead of you on the opposite side of Quentin Rd., but you can follow this path through the preserves until you find a place to cross the road.
Hours	Sunrise to sunset
Distance from station to trailhead	About 3 miles, primarily along the Palatine Trail, which offers bike and walking access away from the street and into Deer Grove Forest Preserves.

Miles of trails	15.5
Acres	2,000
Difficulty	★★★★
In-park recreation options	Hiking, cross-country skiing, ice skating, picnicking, birding, sledding, fishing, bicycling (including rentals at Deer Grove East), model airplane flying (Deer Grove East), drone flying (Deer Grove East), camping, glamping, backpacking
Amenities	Picnic tables and shelters, bathrooms, water
Safety concerns	The trails are roughly maintained and may include roots or other obstructions. They can become mushy after rain.
Plants	Deer Grove is primarily thick oak woodland, while Deer Grove East has a substantive and beautiful prairie landscape.
Water	Deer Grove Lake, where anglers can catch largemouth bass, black bullhead, and bluegill.
Accessibility	Camp Reinberg has an accessible indoor bathroom. Large cabins have a private, accessible, restrooms with a toilet, shower, and two sinks. Deer Grove's trails have varied types of pavement. Some are wide, largely flat, and paved with crushed gravel.
Dogs	Yes—on leashes only
Bikes	This is a very bike friendly park but there are some trails where only foot traffic is allowed. Seasonal bike rentals are available at Deer Grove East.
Family-friendly	Because the trails in this park are more roughly maintained, and because the walk from the train station to the trailhead is so long, this is not a great one for families with small children.
Nearby restaurants	There are a handful of restaurants, cafes, and bars just southeast of the Palatine Metra station.

Barrington: Baker's Lake Nature Preserve

Bring binoculars to this one, it's for the birds. View the island rookery most clearly from the north end of the lake, where there is a viewing platform. The rookery is made of several wooden structures, with three nesting platforms each. It looks a little like scaffolding, but it's exactly the kind of apartment structure that really speaks to a heron's preferred lifestyle. In June at the height of breeding season, it gets downright cacophonous.

The Forest Preserves of Cook County's wildlife division studies this heron population every year, to monitor and maintain the health of the bids and the environment. The birds are banded, which allows scientists to track their movements and learn about where they go when they migrate away during winter. The structure was built in 2000 to provide extra nesting space for endangered and threatened birds, so human intervention isn't wholly unheard of at this site. Recycled Christmas trees are added each year to give extra cover for the very private breed of night herons that nest here.

Other birds you might see here during the year include great blue herons, egrets, cormorants, ducks, mergansers, geese coots (which look like ducks but are more closely related to sandhill cranes), pied-billed grebes, horned grebes, ring-necked ducks, scaups, wigeons, buffleheads, common loons, northern shovelers, gadwalls, and blue-winged teals. There's also a good chance you'll see northern harriers, woodpeckers and coyotes taking advantage of this protected area's habitat.

Follow the path around the lake, through Baker's Lake Nature Preserve, Baker's Lake Younghusband Prairie and enjoy about three miles of trails. Treat it like an out-and-back hike and return the way you came.

Park name	Baker's Lake Nature Preserve
Train station	Barrington
Train line	Metra: Union Pacific Northwest
Schedule	Monday–Friday: departs Chicago as early as 5:55 a.m. and departs Barrington as late as 12:28 a.m. Saturday: departs Chicago as early as 7:00 a.m. and departs Barrington as late as 10:18 p.m. Sundays and holidays: departs Chicago as early as 8:23 a.m. and departs Barrington as late as 9:18 p.m.
Departs from	Ogilvie Transportation Center
Round-trip travel costs	$15.50 full fare, $7.75 reduced fare
Entrance	From the Barrington Metra station head southeast and take a left on South Spring St., take another left onto East Russel St., which will become East Bristol Dr. Take a right onto Queens Cove, another right towards East Hillside Avenue and then continue straight onto South Eastern Ave./East Hillside Ave. The lake will be directly ahead on the right.
Hours	Sunrise to sunset
Distance from station to trailhead	About 1 mile
Miles of trails	About 3
Acres	219
Difficulty	★★
In-park recreation options	Birding, hiking, walking. Fishing not allowed.
Amenities	Hiking and walking trails

Safety concerns	Flooding can be a concern if the weather has been wet.
Animals	Baker's Lake forest preserve is home to one of the most significant heron rookeries in the Midwest.
Plants	Baker's Lake
Water	Restored oak savannah
Accessibility	The paths are largely flat without much grading, and are wide and paved in crushed gravel.
Dogs	Sorry, no.
Bikes	Yes—this park is bike friendly.
Family-friendly	This is a good one especially for families with kids who are curious about birds.
Nearby restaurants	There are plentiful cafes, bars, and restaurants in Barrington, most of them are concentrated around the intersection of Hough St. and Main St., which is just slightly northwest from the train station.

Barrington: Cuba Marsh Forest Preserve

This hike takes you through some scenic residential areas, before leading you into a robust forest system and a diverse marsh and prairie. Access the path to Cuba Marsh Forest Preserve through Citizen Park, a forty-five-acre park managed by the city of Barrington. In the early part of its history Citizen Park was home to the Jewel Tea Company; today it preserves the natural character of the woodland, trails, and waterfalls of the landscape. This is a beautiful park that accents the native character of the wetlands and features beautiful sculptures along the paths. Take a meandering stroll through if you're not in a hurry to get to Cuba Marsh. Check out the Pepper Family Tree House for an accessible and exciting view from the treetops. Come in summer to get up close and personal with the local birds that live in the canopy.

When you exit, you'll find the path to Cuba Marsh Forest Preserve on the northeast side of Citizen's Park. The three miles of trails in Cuba Marsh Forest Preserve take visitors through gently rolling hills, scattered groves, and past beautiful views of the marsh. The trail connecting to Citizens Park includes a boardwalk and a fifty-foot-long timber bridge. Beavers can be spotted here.

In the 1850s settlers came to this land, broke the prairie, and drained the marsh. In the 1950s and 60s most farmers sold their land to developers, but a devoted group of local citizens worked to have it named a preserve governed by the Lake County Forest Preserve. The prairie is especially on display here, and there's a gorgeous boardwalk that lets you walk at the tops of the tallgrasses.

Today many kinds of plants and animals call this preserve home and a wetland offers refuge for waterfowl. There is a unique dry-hill prairie on the southeast side that supports rare plants. The surrounding area was all turned into farmland over time, except for the southeastern corner, which makes it a rare gem for the region. The north branch of the trail in this park leads through rolling oak forests. It's easy to spot migrating birds and raptors in this part of the park.

The water that flows through the marshes flows into nearby Flint Creek, which lets out into the Fox River. The area also collects rainwater and floodwater, keeping it out of homes. Lake County is currently working to replant 80,000 trees within the forest preserve, while removing invasive and nonnative species. In the center of the park you'll come across a stand of pine trees all planted in straight lines. These trees were planted by a former landowner and are not a natural forest but do help prevent soil erosion and provide some habitat for wildlife.

Visitors will have no trouble spotting birds, especially at the edges where the woodland meets the prairies and marshes. Waterfowl, including pied-billed grebes and American coots can be spotted on the wetlands on the southeastern side.

The decision to connect the two parks really opened the trail options here, and these two parks are popular with trail runners looking to get in some mileage. It's also a beautiful spot with stunning views of the surrounding landscape. If you're looking to snag a great pic for Instagram, check out the boardwalk over the marsh. It's hard to overstate how downright pretty this park is.

Park name	**Cuba Marsh Forest Preserve and Citizen Park**
Train station	Barrington
Train line	Metra: Union Pacific Northwest
Schedule	Monday–Friday: departs Chicago as early as 5:55 a.m. and departs Barrington as late as 12:28 a.m. Saturday: departs Chicago as early as 7:00 a.m. and departs Barrington as late as 10:18 p.m. Sundays and holidays: departs Chicago as early as 8:23 a.m. and departs Barrington as late as 9:18 p.m.
Departs from	Ogilvie Transportation Center
Round-trip travel costs	$15.50 full fare, $7.75 reduced fare
Entrance	From the Barrington Metra station head east onto Klingenberg Lane, take another left onto Northwest Highway. Take a right onto Barry Road and follow it around the library. The entrance to Citizen's Park will be here. Take a right, then a left and follow the path ahead until you come to the northeast corner of the park There will be a path ahead of you leading directly into the Cuba Marsh Forest Preserve.
Hours	6:30 am to sunset
Distance from station to trailhead	About 1.5 miles
Miles of trails	About 3
Acres	781
Difficulty	★★★

In-park recreation options	Hiking, biking, cross-country, skiing
Amenities	Picnic tables, public parking, toilets
Safety concerns	Year-round ticks can be a concern at this park.
Plants	Woodland and grassland—tallgrass prairies really shine here
Water	Marshes and prairies—this one is for beautiful vistas
Accessibility	The paths here are between 8' and 14' wide and largely flat. They are primarily made of gravel and can become mushy in the wet months. The terrain is gently rolling with few steep inclines.
Dogs	Yes—on leashes only
Bikes	Yes—this park is bike friendly
Family-friendly	The distance from the trailhead makes this one tough for families with small kiddos, but the activities in Citizen Park are very family oriented.
Nearby restaurants	There are many cafes, bars, and restaurants in Barrington, most of them concentrated around the intersection of Hough St. and Main St., which is just slightly northwest of the train station.

Crystal Lake: Veteran's Acres and Sterne's Woods and Fen

Veteran's Woods and Sterne's Woods and Fen is a great place for beautiful hikes through gently rolling hills, thick stands of oak, aspen, and ash trees, low-lying wetlands with grasses that are taller than you, and a vibrant prairie filled with wildlife. The trailhead is directly next to the Crystal Lake Park District Nature Center, and a ten-minute walk from the Crystal Lake Metra station.

From the Crystal Lake Metra station turn right until you get to Main St. At Main St., take a left past shop and through a residential neighborhood. Carefully cross Route 179; the parking lot for the Crystal Lake Park District Nature Center will be directly ahead of you on the left.

The nature center should be the first stop for any visitor to this park. Get a map, there are a lot of illegal, outdated, or deer paths in this park (especially in the prairie) and it can be easy to go off the trail.

The nature center sits at the top of a hill overlooking a pond. There is a beautiful bridge path around the pond, with some ancient willow trees, but it can get quite mushy if the water is high. Don't be afraid to turn back around if the mud gets to be too much for you. There are also overlook platforms that can be accessed by ramps at the top of the hill.

Visit the nature center to learn about the animals and plants in the park. Veteran's Acres is home to the Wingate Prairie, which is a designated Illinois State Nature Preserve. Visiting the Wingate Prairie gives a modern-day glimpse into what Illinois looked like before the nineteenth century and the invention of the steel plow. A previous landowner tried to turn the area into a Christmas tree farm in the mid-twentieth century; as a result a stand of pines juts oddly from the center of the prairie. The dense grasses native to the area are slowly reclaiming that land. Today, the prairie is home to protected species of butterflies and plants.

At the end of the last Ice Age, this area was left with some pretty sizable rocks, many of them quite near the surface, which makes them easy to spot. These rocks, which can be as small as a pebble or as large as a small car, were carried from sometimes thousands of miles away by mile-thick sheets of ice as they receded from the region roughly 10,000 years ago.

Moving past Wingate Prairie and further into the park, you will encounter a row of power lines running over a wide ribbon of prairie. If you follow the path to the right, you can join up with the Prairie Trail bike path, which will net you access to 56 miles of trail north to Wisconsin. If you continue straight, underneath the power lines, you will come to Sterne's Woods and Fen.

Sterne's Woods is notably hillier than Veteran's Acres. There is the steep slope of a moraine between the woods and the fen. If the idea of ending your hike up a steep, long, uphill climb that will have your hamstrings screaming sounds appealing to you, take a right and follow the path through the woods and gently slope down to the low-lying fen. As you return to the trailhead, you'll come upon a quarter mile march up a steep incline. If that does not sound appealing, take a left and head down the hill first, letting gravity do the work for you. The trail is a loop, so if you go either left or right you will follow the same path and end back at this spot.

When you return, head back across the prairie in the direction of Veteran's Acres. This time choose a different path than the one you came in on and take in a little more of the surrounding woods and prairie. The trails all converge back at the entrance to Wingate Prairie, which you passed on your way in. Visit during the late afternoon hours and you'll probably get to see tons of birds feeding on the seeds found among the prairie grasses.

Park name	Veteran's Acres and Sterne's Woods and Fen
Train station	Crystal Lake
Train line	Metra: Union Pacific Northwest
Schedule	Monday–Friday: departs Chicago as early as 5:55 a.m. and departs Crystal Lake as late as 12:10 a.m. Saturday: departs Chicago as early as 8:30 a.m. and departs Crystal Lake as late as 10:00 p.m. Sunday: and holidays: departs Chicago as early as 8:30 a.m. and departs Crystal Lake as late as 9:03 p.m.
Departs from	Ogilvie Transportation Center
Round-trip travel costs	$18 full fare, $9 reduced
Entrance	From the Crystal Lake Metra head towards Main St. and take a left when you get there. Cross Terra Cotta Ave. and enter the park. The nature center will be in front of you.
Hours	8 a.m. to sunset
Distance from station to trailhead	Less than .5 miles
Miles of trails	Roughly 5 miles within the parks
Acres	Roughly 300 acres of prairie, woodland, savannah, and fen (low-lying, alkaline wetlands)
Difficulty	★★★
In-park recreation options	Geocaching, biking, hiking/running, cross-country skiing, snowshoeing, nature programs and interpretive information
Amenities	Restrooms are available at the nature center and near the parking lot adjacent to the fen. There are no concessions available within the park.
Safety concerns	Year-round, ticks can be a concern.

Plants	Within the space of this park you can see flora in bloom all season. Woodland florals start to appear in early April and May, by June the canopy has grown in and the florals can be found in the prairies and fens for the rest of the season. Native orchids can be found in the fen.
	In 2018 the park completed an initiative to remove invasive buckthorn from the area surrounding the fen. With state assistance park officials removed the plant, raised the creek channels, and reintroduced fire to the landscape. The following year native plants like Joe Pye weed began to reappear.
Water	There are two major water features in this park. In front of the nature center is a pond with beautiful willows, waterfowl, and a fishing pier. The pond is a natural feature, but it also collects stormwater to protect the surrounding neighborhood during heavy rain. There is a walking path around the pond, but it can get flooded. The city of Crystal Lake is currently working to add accessible parking to the side of the pond, which should make it easier for those with mobility concerns to get around.
	The fen is located on the north side of the park. A fen has alkaline water, which allows for different plant species to take root, and it does drain so water doesn't stagnate. These conditions give rare plants like native Illinois orchids a chance to take root. There are only about 200 acres of this type of wetland left in Illinois.
Geology	When the glaciers receded from this area 10,000-odd years ago, they left behind huge glacial erratics in some of the lower-lying prairie regions. Wingate Prairie and the surrounding woodlands sit on top of a moraine, which is a steep hill carved by the glaciers as they receded. When the glaciers melted, the ice released boulders and rocks that had previously been carried from sometimes thousands of miles away and deposited them among the thick clay and glacial till where Wingate Prairie grows now. Many of these erratics can be seen in the prairie from the trails.

	When it rains, water drains through the topsoil and down to an impenetrable layer of clay underground. From there, it flows northwest until it hits the steep slope of the moraines. From there, the groundwater comes out in seeps along the side of the hill and collects in the low-lying fen. As it does this it becomes more alkaline because of the crushed limestone in the soil, which allows the fen to take shape.
Accessibility	Parts of the park are accessible, especially the area around the nature center and pond. The trails can become hilly and steep but are often wide and flat. Between the two parks the trail intersects with the Prairie Trail bike path, which is paved.
Dogs	Yes—on leashes only
Bikes	Yes—this park is bike friendly
Family-friendly	This is a great option for families, but trails can be more difficult so consider that if your kiddo rides in a stroller.
Nearby restaurants	There are a pretty sizable number of cafes, bars, restaurants, and shops in the downtown area surrounding the train station. If you're in a hurry, the café inside the train station sells coffee and baked goods for the train ride back.

Woodstock: Emricson Park

Emricson Park is a sizeable, activity-centric neighborhood park, with no shortage of opportunities for sports and recreation. Hikers will want to enter along the South St. entrance and take the path to the right, which will lead you around the perimeter of the park. Visitors will first travel around the ponds. Continuing along the path, you'll notice a change in elevation as you begin to climb the hill towards the wooded path.

The path guides you past a wooded area with a pond below, around the softball fields and the aquatic center. When you pass the soccer field, look on the other side of the path to see a stand of prairie grasses. Continue following the path past the open fields and volleyball courts and you'll be rewarded with a stand of unbroken woodlands with several different short nature paths through this corner of the park. Explore and return to the main path when you're through. Follow the path past more softball fields and you can exit from the South St. entrance.

Bonus Hike: Want to turn a nice, easy stroll through Emricson Park into an adventure hike with all the best natural spaces Woodstock has to offer in one day? Hike from here to Ryder's Woods Park. The path takes you through another park and down a residential street with sidewalks for most of the way; you'll enter Ryder's Woods on the Kimball Ave. side, and add one and a half miles to your hike.

Directions: Exit Emricson Park via South St. and walk directly across the road (look for traffic, please.) Follow Tara Drive for about 100 feet until you see the entrance for William C. Donato Conservation Area. Within the conservation area, there are not many trails but there is an overlook deck for viewing the marsh and woods below. Deer, birds, beavers, and foxes can be spotted here. The trails are narrow and not ADA-compliant. This little path will take you a short walk through a thirty-acre site that has really only come under serious protection in the last twenty years. When you exit the Conservation Area take a right onto Gerry St. and follow the sidewalk until you come to Kimball Ave., take a left. The entrance to Ryder Woods will be on the left.

Park name	Emricson Park
Train station	Woodstock
Train line	Metra: Union Pacific Northwest
Schedule	Monday–Friday: departs Chicago as early as 5.55 a.m. and departs Woodstock as late as 8:48 p.m. Saturday: departs Chicago as early as 8:30 a.m. and departs Woodstock as late as 9:48 p.m. Sundays and holidays: departs Chicago as early as 9:30 a.m. and departs Woodstock as late as 8:48 p.m.
Departs from	Ogilvie Transportation Center
Round-trip travel costs	$19 full fare, $9.50 reduced
Entrance	Leave the Woodstock Metra station and head south on Main St. Take a right onto Cass St, another left onto Throop St. and a right onto South St. The park will be ahead on the left.
Hours	5 a.m.–11 p.m. (or 15-minutes after the end of a city-approved recreational event).
Distance from station to trailhead	About 1 mile.
Miles of trails	1.75
Acres	160
Difficulty	★★

In-park recreation options	Walking, swimming, tennis, baseball, soccer, volleyball, basketball, sledding hill
Amenities	Pavilion, restrooms, warming houses, playgrounds
Safety concerns	Ticks can be a concern year-round.
Plants	Emricson Park is known for its old-growth oak trees.
Water	Several ponds are present year-round on the western edge of the park.
Accessibility	The paths are wide and paved with concrete. There are some mild changes in elevation.
Dogs	Yes—on leashes only
Bikes	Yes—this park is very bike friendly
Family-friendly	This variety of amenities in this park makes it a great option for families that enjoy lots of sports and other outdoors activities.
Nearby restaurants	Downtown Woodstock is a vibrant place with plenty of restaurants, bars, and cafes along Church St. and through the Woodstock Square Historic District, just south of the Metra station.

Woodstock: Ryder's Wood Park

Ryder's Woods Park is a small but stunning example of how a city can protect its more valuable natural resources and really allow them to flourish. Just twenty-three acres in size, you'll be surprised how much beautiful landscape exists within this park. Ryder's Woods came to exist because activists lobbied the city of Woodstock to buy and protect the property. Today work is still being done to remove invasive species, but what is found there now is abundant displays of flora and fauna.

Visit any season and hikers will find towering white and bur oaks, Virginia creepers, starry false solomon seal, shagbark hickory, willows, and cottonwoods. In the summer visitors will find jewelweeds, poison ivy, and a vibrant rainbow of wildflowers. Sit by the side of the pond and you might just catch flycatchers looking for a meal or see mallards swimming near the island.

Check in on Ryder's Woods in the springtime for a stunning floral display, including Jack-in-the-Pulpit, columbine, and phlox. Warblers are easy to spot here, and robins are abundant, and during the spring and fall migratory seasons this place comes alive with birdsong. Milkweed is plentiful in the meadow, which makes this an easy place to spot butterflies in the warm months.

Park name	Ryder's Woods Park
Train station	Woodstock
Train line	Metra: Union Pacific Northwest
Schedule	Monday–Friday: departs Chicago as early as 5.55 a.m. and departs Woodstock as late as 8:48 p.m. Saturday: departs Chicago as early as 8:30 a.m. and departs Woodstock as late as 9:48 p.m. Sunday and holidays: departs Chicago as early as 9:30 a.m. and departs Woodstock as late as 8:48 p.m.
Departs from	Ogilvie Transportation Center

Round-trip travel costs	$19 full fare, $9.50 reduced
Entrance	From the Woodstock Metra station head southeast on Wheeler St., take a left onto Church St. Take a right onto Jefferson St. and a left onto Fremont St. Turn right onto Lawndale Ave., the entrance to Ryder's Woods will be at the end of the street.
Hours	Dawn to dusk
Distance from station to trailhead	A little less than 1 mile
Miles of trails	About 1 mile
Acres	About 23 within the park; the trail travels through about 10 of them.
Difficulty	★★
In-park recreation options	Walking, Interpretive information
Amenities	Few within this small park.
Safety concerns	The terrain is roughly maintained and can be a trip hazard.
Plants	Thick stands of deep oak woods
Water	Vernal pools and ponds
Accessibility	This park is not ADA-compliant. Trails are roughly maintained, narrow, and have varied terrain.
Dogs	Yes—on leashes only
Bikes	Due to the small size of the park and the rough terrain, this park is not very bike-friendly.
Family-friendly	This is a great option for families with kids of all ages.
Nearby restaurants	Jefferson St. runs straight through the heart of the Woodstock Square Historic District, which is full of cafes, bars, and restaurants.

MILWAUKEE DISTRICT WEST TO ELGIN

River Grove: Des Plaines River Trail, Schiller Park

The abundance of recreation options here is something to note. There are at least seventeen miles of continuous trails, a model airplane flying field (drones are allowed), and hiking trails through oak woodlands. There's no shortage of trails, some of them quite challenging.

Hikers will have no trouble spotting deer, including bucks with impressive antlers. Birdwatchers will spot great horned owls and winter wrens, as well as American tree sparrows, brown creepers, black-capped chickadees, and Cooper's hawks.

Visitors to Schiller Woods East will also find a pocket of remnant prairie, sage meadow, and wetlands with colorful plants and insects. The unpaved Brown Trail of the Des Plains Trail System is accessed through this park.

Anglers will want to check out Schiller Pond. It's shallow, with a maximum depth of just over six feet. Seven bump-outs make it easy to access the deeper waters. This pond is stocked with largemouth bass, bluegill, channel catfish, and hybrid sunfish.

Near Irving Park Rd. inside the park, you might see people carrying massive empty water jugs to fill them up from a hand pump in the park. Local legend, and people take this seriously, is that the water from this hand pump has healing and restorative properties that water found in surrounding fountains or pumps does not. The Forest Preserves of Cook County officially will not confirm that this is true, but that doesn't stop the true believers from coming. Some say it just plain tastes better. Others will tell you that Pope John Paul II personally blessed the pump when he visited Chicago in 1979, though there is no record of this. Fill up your water bottle here and test the magic for yourself.

Park name	Schiller Park
Train station	River Grove
Train line	Metra: Milwaukee District West
Schedule	Monday–Friday: departs Chicago as early as 5:39 a.m. and departs River Grove as late as 10:58 p.m. Saturday: departs Chicago as early as 7:30 a.m. and departs River Grove as late as 10:58 p.m. Sunday: departs Chicago as early as 8:30 a.m. and departs River Grove as late as 10:55 p.m.
Departs from	Union Station
Round-trip travel costs	$11 full fare, $5.50 reduced
Entrance	From the River Grove Metra station head south on Thatcher Ave. and take a right onto Arnold St. Arnold will become Indian Boundary Rd. after it takes a left. Take another right onto Grand Ave. and the entrance to the Des Plaines River Trail will be on your right.
Hours	Sunrise—sunset
Distance from station to trailhead	About .5 miles
Miles of trails	The Des Plaines River Trail has about 30 miles of continuous trail.
Acres	The Des Plaines River Trail includes about 13,000 acres of vegetation, wetlands, and paths.
Difficulty	★★
In-park recreation options	Hiking, biking, picnicking, cross-country skiing, canoeing, fishing, model airplane flying, Indian Boundary Golf Course
Amenities	Portable bathroom, picnic shelter, public golf course

Safety concerns	The Des Plaines River Trail currently breaks for the Union Pacific Railroad crossing between Golf Road and Central Avenue. Crossing is prohibited for safety reasons. The Forest Preserves of Cook County has plans to build a footbridge here, but a completion date is not set. Since you cannot safely cross the river at this level, cross via the pedestrian crosswalk at Bender and Golf roads. You will be able to rejoin the trail on the other side. Seasonal flooding is common in the sections of the path between Touhy and North avenues. Depending on the weather and conditions parts of the trail, particularly underpasses, may have standing water.
Water	This trail runs alongside the Des Plaines River, which means that flooding is an issue.
Accessibility	The trail is stone, generally flat, and does not include any stairs or steep elements. However, it can have roots or debris that can leave it with less than the standard 10' width. An accessible indoor restroom is available at Schiller Woods—East.
Dogs	Yes—on leashes only
Bikes	Yes—this park is bike friendly
Family-friendly	Yep, the variety of activities and distance to the train station makes this a good option for families.
Nearby restaurants	You'll find no shortage of restaurants around Grand Ave. along the edge of the park. There is a nearby diner and tiki bar, if you're feeling festive after your hike. Want something quick and classic? Legendary Gene & Jude's hot dog stand is right there.

Itasca: Springbrook Nature Center

This is a great one for families and the stroller crowd. The path from the train to the entrance to the park is about one-half mile down a footpath, completely separated from traffic. Once you enter the Springbrook Nature Center you can choose to either wander the trails, observing the beautiful and varied landscape, or you can enter the nature center itself. The nature center occupies a red barn that's been on the property here for over a century. Today, it houses information about the surrounding area, and nine raptors who live outside the nature center year-round.

Follow the Riverwalk Path from the Itasca Metra station to the Springbrook Nature Center and enjoy a half-mile, paved stroll through a natural setting, separated from traffic. When you get to the nature center, you'll find two miles of trails, with excellent wayfinding and a scenic setting. Outside around the center it's common to spot hawks, owls, and turkey vultures. If you keep your eyes a little closer to the ground, you might spot deer, beaver, mink, coyotes, turtles, and raccoons.

The Springbrook Nature Center is a home for injured raptors including red-tailed hawks, turkey vultures, owls and kestrels. This is a great place to get up-close-and-personal with some of the coolest birds that exist anywhere in the world.

Bonus hike: If you've seen all the gorgeous scenery surrounding the Springbrook Nature Center, but you're not quite ready to go home, you can take a short (.7 mile) walk through a cute residential neighborhood to the Songbird Slough Nature Preserve.

Exit the nature center at Valley Rd. and take a right on Lombard Ave. Enter the Songbird Slough Forest Preserve at Oak Ave. and follow the path through the low-lying wetlands. This is one of the best places for birding in this corner of Chicagoland.

Park name	Springbrook Nature Center
Train station	Itasca
Train line	Metra: Milwaukee District West
Schedule	Monday–Friday: departs Chicago as early as 5:39 a.m. and departs Itasca at 10:43 p.m. Saturday: departs Chicago as early as 7:30 and departs Itasca as late as 10:38 p.m. Sunday: departs Chicago as early as 8:39 a.m. and departs Itasca as late as 1:22 a.m.
Departs from	Union Station
Round-trip travel costs	Full fare $13.50, reduced $6.75
Entrance	From the Itasca Metra station go right on Orchard St., take another right onto Walnut St., cross over Spring Brook and follow the path to the Springbrook Nature Center.
Hours	Springbrook Nature Center (indoors): Open seasonally. Springbrook Nature Center (trails): Open sunrise-sunset.
Distance from station to trailhead	About .5 miles on a footpath that is completely separate from traffic for large parts of the journey.
Miles of trails	About 2
Acres	127
Difficulty	★
In-park recreation options	Hiking and birdwatching, snowshoeing, large indoor aquarium, butterfly garden and hummingbird garden, fishing pond, pool and splash pad
Amenities	Wayfinding signage, seasonal indoor restroom facilities

Safety concerns	Ticks are common here.
Water	The Springbrook Nature Center occupies a piece of land that has historically been a floodplain. Today, ecologists use this space to restore native plants to the region and collect rainwater that would otherwise end up in people's basements.
Accessibility	The trails here are wide, flat, paved, and very well maintained. The Springbrook Nature Center has an indoor facility that is accessible.
Dogs	Yes—on leashes under ten feet only
Bikes	Yes—this park is bike friendly
Family-friendly	This park is accessible from a short, protected path from the station and is full of information and activities for small kids.
Nearby restaurants	Downtown Itasca is a vibrant community with plenty of shops, cafes, bars, and restaurants just north of the train station, mostly around Walnut Street.

Itasca: Songbird Slough Forest Preserve

If you've seen all the gorgeous scenery surrounding the Springbrook Nature Center, but you're not quite ready to go home, you can add some mileage and see a stunning lake in the Songbird Slough Forest Preserve. Songbird Slough is a mix of natural and constructed wetlands, restored prairies, meadows and Songbird Lake.

Enter the Songbird Slough Forest Preserve at Oak Ave. and follow the path through the low-lying wetlands. You will enter just north of a three-way intersection in the park. A road does run through the main park area, so please use caution and watch for traffic. You can either head straight ahead, to find Songbird Lake, or you can take a tour of the area by taking the path either to the right or left.

This is one of the best places for birding in this corner of Chicagoland. Birds call these grasslands home during the warmer seasons, while Songbird Lake provides vital fishing and nesting opportunity for over 200 kinds of birds. The Illinois Natural Areas Inventory has recognized Songbird Slough for its unique features, and potential to help re-establish nearly 100 species of endangered or threatened birds. Among the species spotted here, visitors may see savannah sparrows, American woodcocks, marsh wrens, spotted sandpipes, warbling vireos, bobolinks, and hooded mergansers.

The slough was formed when the Wisconsin Glacier receded thousands of years ago, forming a shallow lake. The southern fourteen acres of the lake are remnants of this natural slough. Fishing is allowed in Songbird Lake, and a lucky angler might catch one of the stocked largemouth bass, bluegill, channel catfish, crappie, and northern pike in this lake. Fishing licenses are required here, where applicable.

Songbird Slough has a pretty interesting glacial history. When the Wisconsin Glacier retreated to the northeast tens of thousands of years ago, a large chunk broke off, and became partially buried in sediment. As the ice melted, it left a depression that filled with water from the melting glacier. This was the beginning of Songbird Slough. In the 1970s, the DuPage Forest Preserve District began purchasing most of the land the slough sits on today.

Park name	Songbird Slough Forest Preserve
Train station	Itasca
Train line	Metra: Milwaukee District West
Schedule	Monday–Friday: departs Chicago as early as 5:39 a.m. and departs Itasca at 10:43 p.m. Saturday: departs Chicago as early as 7:30 and departs Itasca as late as 10:38 p.m. Sunday: departs Chicago as early as 8:39 a.m. and departs Itasca as late as 1:22 a.m.
Departs from	Union Station
Round-trip travel costs	Full fare $13.50, reduced $6.75
Entrance	From the Itasca Metra station go right on Orchard St., take another right onto Walnut St., turn right onto the Itasca Riverwalk until you come to Maple St., take a left. Take another right onto Bloomingdale Rd., and a left onto Oak St. The entrance to the slough will be ahead of you.
Hours	Year round from one hour after sunrise until one hour after sunset.
Distance from station to trailhead	About .75 miles through mostly residential areas with sidewalks

Miles of trails	About 2 in the Songbird Slough Forest Preserve
Acres	390 in Songbird Slough
Difficulty	★★
In-park recreation options	Hiking, birdwatching, biking, fishing
Amenities	Picnic tables, restrooms
Safety concerns	Ticks are common here.
Water	The Songbird Slough is a remnant of a glacial lake, formed thousands of years ago.
Accessibility	The trails here are wide, flat, paved, and very well maintained. The path along the northern side of the lake is made of turf. There are several unmarked dirt footpaths connecting the main road to the lakeshore.
Dogs	Dogs are allowed on leashes under 10' only.
Bikes	Yes—this park is bike friendly
Family-friendly	This park is near to the train station and a good option for families with kids interested in birds or fish.
Nearby restaurants	Downtown Itasca is a vibrant community with plenty of shops, cafes, bars, and restaurants just north of the train station, mostly around Walnut Street.

Hanover Park: Mallard Lake and Hawk Hollow Forest Preserve

The easiest way to enter Mallard Lake is from Greenbrook Ave., through the path from the Heritage Park entrance, which has a path leading directly into the Mallard Lake Forest Preserve. Heritage Park is a community park, with playgrounds, a sledding hill, basketball courts, and a fishing pond. Follow the path and you will enter Mallard Lake Forest Preserve through a wooded path, which leads to the lakes themselves.

Enter this trail system on the north side of Mallard Lake Forest Preserve. This preserve has open waters, wetlands, fields, and scattered woodlands that provide a home for beavers, great blue herons, bullfrogs, eastern meadowlarks, bobolinks, red-tailed hawks, and kestrels. Follow the trails to your left as you enter the park and you'll wind around the 85-acre lake. The trails are wide, paved with crushed gravel, and without much steep grade to them. More roughly maintained footpaths snake the shores of the lakes. There are at least four miles of trails surrounding Mallard Lake, including two bridges that will carry you onto the islands within the lake.

Want more mileage in your hike today? Return to the spot where the path split off, just after you left Heritage Park. Follow the other path and you will connect with the Hawk Hollow Forest Preserve. Here you'll find grassy meadows, mature woodlands, and fens with the beautiful west branch of the DuPage River running through the middle of it all. This preserve is one of the largest unbroken blocks of grassland habitats in Kane County and is home to several uncommon bird species, including Henslow's sparrows, grasshopper sparrows, and savanna sparrows.

Got the kind of pooch who would run in circle all day if you'd let them? Hawk Hollow has a thirty-four-acre, fully fenced off-leash dog park with separate areas for large and small dogs. You will need to carry proof of a valid Forest Preserve District permit for each dog.

Continue following the trails in the park west and turn south at Bartlett Rd. Take a left at Schick Rd. and re-enter the trail systems just west of Gerber Rd. You'll be able to access the West Branch Forest Preserve here. This preserve features two lakes, a reservoir, wetlands, tallgrass meadows, wet prairies, immature floodplain forests, and a rare fen full of reptiles, amphibians, mammals, and birds.

The forty-acre Deep Quarry Lake has two fishing piers and allows a maximum depth of forty-five feet, if you're really angling for one of those big bottom feeders. Night fishing is allowed here, but anglers must be out by 11 p.m. Bluegill, bass, sunfish, channel and flathead catfish, carp, and crappie are all common here.

Park name	Mallard Lake (with bonus hike to Hawk Hollow Forest Preserve)
Train station	Hanover Park
Train line	Metra: Milwaukee District West
Schedule	Monday–Friday: departs downtown as early as 5:39 a.m. and departs Hanover Park as late as 10:29 p.m. Saturday: departs downtown as early as 7:30 a.m. and departs Hanover Park as late as 1:37 a.m. Sunday: departs downtown as early as 8:30 a.m. and departs Hanover Park as late as 10:23 a.m.
Round-trip travel costs	$14.50 full fare, $7.25 reduced
Entrance	From the Hanover street Metra station exit and head south by turning right onto County Farm Road. Take a left onto Arlington Drive and a right onto Barrington Road. The Entrance to the Mallard Lake Forest Preserve will be directly ahead of you.

Hours	Open daily from an hour after sunrise to an hour after sunset.
Distance from station to trailhead	About 1.75 miles
Miles of trails	About 12
Acres	Not quite 3,000
Difficulty	★★★
In-park recreation options	Hiking, picnicking, fishing, off-leash dog area (Hawk Hollow)
Amenities	Vault toilets, portable toilets
Safety concerns	Trails can become muddy when the weather has been wet. Flooding is an occasional concern around Mallard Lake.
Plants	Hawk Hollow has a beautiful and extensive prairie system, with grassy meadows, mature woodlands, and fens.
Water	Mallard Lake is home to 3 different ponds, 2 islands and a creek.
Accessibility	Mallard Lake has 2 wheelchair accessible piers. The trails are wide, largely flat, and paved with crushed gravel. They can become mushy when weather has been wet.
Dogs	Yes—on leash only
Bikes	Yes—this park is very bike friendly
Family-friendly	Very. Several playgrounds are accessible from the Hanover Park entrance.
Nearby restaurants	There are some restaurants scattered around Hanover Park, including a few northeast of the train station.

National Street: Fox River Trail

The Fox River Trail is about forty miles of paved and unpaved path that stretches as far north as Algonquin and as far south as Oswego. This path follows primarily alongside the Fox River, crossing over it in several places. In several places between Batavia and North Aurora it splits and runs parallel to both sides of the river. This is one of Illinois' finer examples of a successful rails-to-trails conversion, which allowed long stretches of this path to be built without difficult grade changes. It catches up with some of the more extensive cross-country trails including the Illinois Prairie path, the Great Western Trail, Virgil Gilman Trail, Prairie Trail, and the Grand Illinois Trail.

Enter the Fox River Trail and head north to check out Voyager's Landing, with 2,000 feet of shoreline and excellent fishing. On the opposite side from there, you'll find Trout Park, which represents some of the unique glacial features of the Fox River Valley. These woodlands extend from dry bluff tops, with white and bur oak, to low damp depressions with sugar maple, blue ash, rock elm, and chinquapin oak. On the slopes in between you'll find white ash and witch hazel. The bluffs are framed on either side by two ravines formed by springs and seeps. Come during the summer months to find marsh marigold, American black currant, and great Angelica. This place has been noted for its diverse plant life going back as far as the 1920s and is some of the more beautiful examples of Illinois' native landscape.

If you head towards South Elgin, you'll come to the Jon H. Deurr Forest Preserve. This small preserve is in a crook of the Fox River, with woodlands, fishing, bird watching, and ample stones for skipping (remnants of the old gravel pit hills). Visitors here will find original prairies and exposed rock ledges and outcroppings. Near

Five Islands Park visitors will find the graves of two unknown soldiers who died of cholera while fighting in the Blackhawk War. Most notably here is a pristine (meaning we never altered it, so we never screwed it up, this is all natural) eight-foot-high waterfall that cascades and pools in the clear creek.

Park name	Fox River Trail
Train station	National Street
Train line	Metra: Milwaukee District West
Schedule	Monday–Friday: departs downtown as early as 5:48 a.m. and departs National Street as late as 10:18 p.m. Saturday: departs downtown as early as 7:30 a.m. and departs National Street as late as 10: 12 p.m. Sundays departs downtown as early as 8:30 a.m. and departs National Street as late as 10:12 p.m.
Departs from	Union Station
Round-trip travel costs	$16.50 full fare, $8.25 reduced
Entrance	From the National St. station exit the station and head north. Cross the Fox River at National St. and you will be able to catch up with the Fox River trail immediately on the other side of the river.
Hours	Sunrise to sunset
Distance from station to trailhead	About .25 miles
Miles of trails	About 40
Acres	★★
Difficulty	Hiking, biking, cross-country skiing, jogging

In-park recreation options	Trails, interpretive information, picnic shelters
Amenities	This is a multipurpose trail and popular with walkers, runners, and cyclists. Please use caution on the trail and try to keep slower traffic to the right.
Safety concerns	Along the trail visitors will find woodlands, wetlands, prairies, and islands with a varied landscape along the route.
Water	The Fox River
Accessibility	Most of this trail is ADA-compliant and paved in either asphalt or limestone screenings.
Dogs	Yes—on leashes only
Bikes	Yes—this park is bike friendly
Family-friendly	The distance from the train station and the variety of recreation options makes this a great option for families with kids of all ages.
Nearby restaurants	Restaurants are found alongside National St. but on the other side of the river.

UNION
PACIFIC WEST

River Forest: Thatcher Woods

South of the Des Plaines River Trail, but not officially a part of it, you'll find Thatcher Woods. This preserve has one of the only remaining examples of quality floodplain forest left in this part of the country. Here visitors will find more than 250 species of plants and animals native to the region. Enter from the southern end and you'll walk right into the forest. As you head north, the scenery eventually gives way to river bluffs. Visit in the summertime to see abundant and colorful wildflowers on the prairies. During flooding seasons, the river may be high, creating expanded feeding grounds for great white egrets, turtles, kingfishers, and woodpeckers.

Check out the Hal Tyrrell Trailside Museum north of where you entered for tons of useful information about the area's native animals, wildflower gardens, wildlife, and their habitats. You can even visit with some rescued raptors here, if getting up close with flying predators is your thing. Admission is free.

If you're planning on taking the same Metra back home, turn back around and exit where you came in the park. As you re-enter the southern end of the park, you'll notice the variety of oaks that make up the canopy of the savanna. Swamp white, red, white, and bur oaks are abundant, and share space with native grasses and wildflowers including bloodroot, white trout lily, wild coffee, yellow pimpernel, and spring beauties.

This is a great place to spot some of Chicago's most common birds, the same ones you might spot in your own backyard. Keep an eye out for wood thrushes, great crested flycatchers, scarlet tanager, red-headed woodpeckers, black-billed and yellow-billed cuckoos, and sharp-skinned, veery, red-shouldered, and broad-winged hawks. If you hear a bird song that sounds like it's calling "tea-*cher* tea-*cher* tea-*cher*," that's the ovenbird's distinctive and musical tone.

Park name	Thatcher Woods
Train station	River Forest
Train line	Metra: Union Pacific West Line
Schedule	Monday–Friday: departs Chicago as early as 5:53 a.m. and departs River Forest as late as 11:17 p.m. Saturday: departs Chicago as early as 8:40 a.m. and departs River Forest as late as 11:25 p.m. Sunday: departs Chicago as early as 8:40 a.m. and departs River Forest as late as 11:25 p.m.
Departs from	Ogilvie Transportation Center
Round-trip travel costs	$8.50 full fare, $4.25 reduced
Entrance	From the River Forest station head west on Hawthorne Ave. and take a right onto Thatcher Rd. Follow that until you come to Chicago Ave., then take a left. The entrance to the trail will be on the right.
Hours	Trails: Sunrise to sunset The Trailside Museum of Natural History just across Chicago Ave. is a year-round nature center with free admission. March–October: 9 a.m.–5 p.m. November–February: 9 a.m.–4 p.m. Closed Fridays, Thanksgiving, Christmas, New Year's Day
Distance from station to trailhead	Less than .5 miles
Miles of trails	5
How many acres?	245
Difficulty	★★

In-park recreation options	Hiking, birding, cycling, picnicking, drone flying, Trailside Museum of Natural History
Amenities	Restrooms, picnic area
Safety concerns	Ticks can be a concern here year round.
Plants	This is a beautiful example of oak woodlands and a floodplain forest.
Water	This trail runs alongside the Des Plaines River, which means that it's flooding can be a concern.
Accessibility	The restrooms are accessible. The trails are wide, largely flat, and paved with crushed gravel.
Dogs	Yes—on leashes only. Dogs are not allowed inside the Hal Tyrrell Trailside Museum or on its grounds.
Bikes	Yes—this park is bike friendly. Bikes are not allowed within the grounds of the Hal Tyrrell Trailside Museum.
Family-friendly	Yes, take your kiddos to visit the Hal Tyrrell Trailside Museum.
Nearby restaurants	There are a handful of restaurants, cafés, and bars on Lake St., on either side of the park.

Geneva: The Fox River Trail

This hike is like a guided history tour, meandering through neighborhoods and regional parks, with stops along the way for notable historical markers, including a Viking ship and Civil War-era training camp. The route doesn't venture too far from town but what it lacks in solitude it makes up for in quality, history, and accessibility.

When you enter the Gunnar Anderson Forest Preserve you will travel down a path and come to a footbridge across the river. Cross here and you will enter Island Park. Beautiful trees line the riverwalk and waterfowl are common. When you cross the second, smaller footbridge you will be on Island Park. Here visitors will find a beautiful pavilion, gardens, and a treehouse-themed playground, including a zipline. Further north there are sculptures of remnant ironwork and gears salvaged from a prominent mill in Geneva's history.

Continue north past the dam on the Fox River Trail you will come to Riverbank Park. Follow the trail inland at Riverbank Park into Good Templar Park, where you can check out a real-life Viking ship that sailed from Norway to Chicago. It then hung out here for the 1893 Chicago World's Fair. After the fair it eventually made its way to this spot in St. Charles where the Friends of the Viking Ship maintain its upkeep. It is open occasionally, so check with the Friends of the Viking Ship for availability (www.vikingship.us).

If you skip the Viking ship, just continue north on the Fox River Trail. If you saw the Viking ship, you can catch back up with the trail by following the path through Good Templar Park the way you came, or catch back up with it on Woodward Ave., just south of the Friends of the Viking Ship's building.

Continue north until you come to Camp Kane. This spot marks the location of the only Civil War training camp in Illinois. During the Civil War soldiers were trained or passed through here. Visitors can now view a few monuments to the camp itself. The city of St. Charles relocated a 14' x 18' building, put up just a few years before the Civil War, to this site. Before the war, the building was the comically tiny office of a local attorney. During the war it held soldiers who had defected. You can still see the graffiti they carved on the interior walls. Camp Kane is open seasonally, but Langum Park in which it sits is open year round.

Here you can turn around and head back to Geneva or continue north. An adventurous hiker might want to keep following the path north until you reach the National Street Metra, where you can catch the Milwaukee District West line back into the city. That hike would be about twelve miles.

Park name	The Fox River Trail—specifically through Gunnar Anderson Forest Preserve, Island Park Bennett Park, and Camp Kane
Train station	Geneva
Train line	Metra: Union Pacific West
Schedule	Monday–Friday: leaves Chicago as early as 5:53 a.m., departs Geneva as late as 1:47 a.m. Saturday: departs Chicago as early as 8:40 a.m., departing Geneva as late as 10:37 a.m. Sunday: departs Chicago as early as 8:40 a.m., departs Geneva as late as 10:37 p.m.
Departs from	Ogilvie Transportation Center
Round-trip travel costs	$16.50 full fare, $8.25 reduced
Entrance	Exit the Geneva Metra station and take a right onto 3rd St. Follow that south until you see the campus for the Kane County Government. The trailhead will be at the intersection of 3rd St. and 1st St.
Hours	Sunrise to sunset

Distance from station to trailhead	Less than .25 miles
Miles of trails	This is more like a guided walking history tour but if you loop in both the Viking Ship and Camp Kane, you're probably looking at a 6-mile round-trip hike to and from the train station. The Fox River Trail includes roughly 40 contiguous miles of multiuse trail.
Acres	About 145
Difficulty	★★
In-park recreation options	Hiking, biking, birding, fishing, kayaking, canoeing
Amenities	Restrooms, picnic shelters, playgrounds
Safety concerns	This trail is directly alongside the Fox River, so flooding can be a concern when the weather has been wet.
Plants	This walk takes you past manicured gardens, wild marshes, and woodlands.
Water	This trail runs along the Fox River.
Geology	The Fox River Watershed formed as a result of the receding and melting of the Wisconsin Glacier 11,000 years ago.
Accessibility	The trail is wide, flat, and paved with few steep grade changes, but it does occasionally cross the road or sidewalk.
Dogs	Yes—on leashes only
Bikes	Yes—it's very bike friendly
Family-friendly	The distance from the train station and the variety of recreation options makes this a great option for families with kids of all ages.
Nearby restaurants	Mostly clustered near State St. This walk passes by wine cellars, galleries, breweries, and spas, so there are plenty of opportunities to refresh yourself off the trail. Fox River Canoe and Kayak also has an outpost right on the river, if you'd prefer to paddle the day away rather than hike.

Elburn: Elburn Forest Preserve

All the way at the end of the line, you'll find the village of Elburn. It's no surprise that more than forty miles west of Chicago, the skyscrapers make way for apartments, which make way for houses, which only intermittently accent the pastoral landscape. Elburn is a farm town and the Elburn Forest Preserve is an oak woodland abutting huge open prairies with big skies above. It's a topographic and woody retreat, in an otherwise agricultural landscape.

When you enter Elburn County Forest Preserve, you'll find yourself at the trailhead surrounded by a beautiful prairie landscape. You can find a map at the trailhead. Follow the path forward and you will join the major loop around the park itself. The wayfinding within the park is fairly good so look for the wooden posts indicating the trails.

Head in either direction for long enough, and you'll come to the Fox River Wildlife Center. The center primarily serves as a wildlife hospital that takes in orphaned, injured or sick wildlife from the surrounding region. There are educational programs at this facility, but its hours are limited.

Just outside of the wildlife center, however, there is a small marker on the side of the path. This marker indicates that the Old Oregon Trail passed through here. This trail, which existed a little before the Oregon Trail that carried all those settlers out west, started in Chicago and eventually met up with what would become that Oregon Trail. Local Boy Scouts have marked the location they were able to verify where the trail crossed through this property.

Ahead on the trail visitors will come to a limestone picnic shelter that was constructed during the Great Depression. It's a pretty shelter, with skylights and beautiful arched windows, facing a wooded landscape. Towards the southern end of the park, especially along the blue paths, topography becomes a little more varied for short parts of the trail.

Park name	Elburn Forest Preserve
Train station	Elburn
Train line	Metra: Union Pacific West
Schedule	Monday–Friday: Departs from Chicago as early as 5:53 a.m. and returns from Elburn as late as 10:18 p.m. Saturday: departs from Chicago as early as 8:40 a.m. and leaves from Elburn as late as 10:25 p.m. Sunday: departs from Chicago as early as 8:40 a.m. and returns from Elburn as late as 10:25 p.m.
Departs from	Ogilvie Transportation Center
Round-trip travel costs	$18 full fare, $9 reduced
Entrance	Exit the Elburn Metra station and take the pedestrian path across the parking lot, heading west on E. Kansas St. Turn right onto S. 1st St. and turn left onto E. North St. Take a slight left onto North Grasslands Trail and the park will be directly ahead of you.
Hours	Sunrise to sunset
Distance from station to trailhead	About .75 miles
Miles of trails	2.25
Acres	168
Difficulty	**
In-park recreation options	Hiking, biking, birding, picnics
Amenities	Picnic shelters, vault toilets
Safety concerns	Trail conditions can get mushy when the weather has been wet.

Plants	This park is home to high-quality oak savannahs and woodland dominated by white, black, and bur oaks, as well as shagbark hickory.
Geology	This park is situated on a morainal, gravel hill at the county watershed divide, which separates the Fox and the Kishwaukee river basins.
Accessibility	The paths are wide and flat with few steep grade changes. The trails can become muddy and damp, especially the mowed paths across open fields. Some paths are made of crushed gravel, while others are paved and both of those are less prone to flooding. Restrooms are found at the trailhead and near the picnic shelter.
Dogs	Yes—on leashes only
Bikes	Yes—this park is very bike friendly
Family-friendly	This one is near the train station and has good wayfinding and a wildlife center so it's a good option for families with kids of all ages.
Nearby restaurants	There are some cafes and restaurants in downtown Elburn.

BNSF RAILWAY

Stone Avenue: Salt Creek Woods, Possum Hollow Wood, and Bemis Woods

When you enter Salt Creek Woods, you'll follow a short path over the Salt Creek and come to a T-intersection. If you take a right, you'll go up into Possum Hollow Woods and head back south through Brezina Woods north of that. You can follow this path all the way to the Brookfield Zoo if you're looking for a big adventure. If instead, at the T you take a left, you will enter the Salt Creek Woods Nature Preserve and Bemis Woods.

Salt Creek Woods is a Nature Preserve comprised of upland oak-dominated woodland, floodplain woods along Salt Creek, and some prairie. Most of the prairies that did exist here are lost, but you can check out a few remaining elements at the Wolf Road Prairie Nature at 31st St. and Wolf Rd.

If instead you continue forward into you park, you'll walk through Bob Mann Woods and eventually come to Wolf Rd. You can take this north and see the prairie or cross Wolf Rd and enter Bemis Woods.

In Bemis Woods there are ample and more-roughly maintained trails, as well as a zipline course. Visit during the summer months and you can whiz along the treetops at the birds' level. The trails here wind and intersect all over the natural landscape. Tall oaks dominate, but closer to the ground prairie grasses compete for sunlight. During the winter, that creates a dynamic landscape full of songbirds and golden grasses.

Adventurous hikers might want to try to get off the train at Western Springs and head north through Bemis Woods. At the intersection of Canterbury Lake and the Tri-State Tollway, you can begin the seven-mile Salt Creek Greenway Trail. This thirteen-and-a-half-mile trail follows the Salt Creek through Bemis Woods, back through the Salt Creek Nature Preserve, north through Possum Hollow

Woods, where it meets up with Brezina Woods, then 26th St. Woods, and—finally—Brookfield Woods. The trail comes to an end near the entrance to the Brookfield Zoo, which is a short half-mile walk to the Hollywood/Zoo Stop. Someone willing to do this could easily hike fifteen miles or more in one day.

Park name	Salt Creek Woods, Possum Hollow Wood, and Bemis Woods
Train station	Stone Avenue
Train line	Metra: BNSF Railway
Schedule	Monday–Friday: departs Chicago as early as 5:14 a.m., leaving Stone Ave. as late as 9:07 p.m. Saturday: it departs Chicago as early as 6:30 a.m. and departs Stone Ave. as late as 9:01 a.m. Sunday: it departs Chicago as early as 8:40 a.m. and departs Stone Ave. as late as 9:01 p.m.
Departs from	Union Station
Round-trip travel costs	$11 full fare, $5.50 reduced
Entrance	From the Stone Ave. train station turn right on Brainerd, follow Brainerd north until you come to Jackson Ave. and the entrance to the park will be on your left.
Hours	Sunrise to sunset
Distance from station to trailhead	About 1 mile
Miles of trails	Salt Creek Trail system connects to Bemis Woods meaning from here you can access 19 miles of trails as far east as Riverside and north towards Roosevelt Rd.
Acres	480 in Bemis Woods alone
Difficulty	★★

In-park recreation options	Hiking, biking
Amenities	Pavilion with fireplace
Safety concerns	Trail conditions can become muddy when the weather is wet.
Animals	Both Bemis Woods North and South are considered excellent birding locations because of the creek habitat. A large variety of migrant songbirds, as well as cuckoos, indigo buntings, and veeries, use this 400-acre wooded area along Salt Creek.
Plants	Most of the area around this trail system is oak woodland, and floodplain with prairie plants. It's really beautiful.
Water	The Salt Creek runs throughout this area.
Animals	Both Bemis Woods North and South are considered excellent birding locations because of the creek habitat. A large variety of migrant songbirds, as well as cuckoos, indigo buntings, and veeries, use this 400-acre wooded area along Salt Creek.
Accessibility	The primary path is wide, flat, and paved with a line down the center indicating the direction of travel. It is in good condition and unlikely to become muddy or mushy during the wet seasons. Footpaths jutting off the main trail are more rustic, more roughly maintained, can be difficult to locate, and are often muddy or wet.
Dogs	Yes—on leashes only
Bikes	Yes—very popular with bikes
Family-friendly	This is a great option for families on bikes, but might be a bit tougher for hiking with small kiddos.
Nearby restaurants	There are plenty of restaurants and cafes clustered around Hillgrove and Burlington avenues. However, if you have the time and inclination walk to the area around the LaGrange Metra station. It's less than one half mile east of the Stove Ave. Metra station, but has a greater variety of restaurants, bars, and cafes.

SOUTHWEST SERVICE AND HERITAGE CORRIDOR

The Big Palos Adventure Camp—From Palos Heights & Palos Park—SouthWest Service to Willow Springs—Heritage Corridor

During the process of writing this book I procrastinated on this chapter. The rich concentration of park space in this region, just west of the Bridgeview neighborhood, bordered by the Des Plaines river on the north, and extending as far south as 143rd St., includes a few dozen individual parks, nature preserves, forest systems, and one campground. Some of these are managed by the Forest Preserves of Cook County, and some of them are managed by local municipalities. The result is the densest concentration of green space you'll find in Cook County. It has three nearby train stops, on two separate train lines, so I had the hope it would be a rich and easily accessible environment for everyone.

Then I sat down to write this chapter and learned that the infrastructure is there, but the trains don't run as often as they could. The Heritage Corridor Line, which has a nearby station in Willow Springs, is a commuter-only train. It runs into Chicago in the morning, and out of Chicago in the evening. If you wanted to head out here from Chicago in the morning, it's not going to happen on the Heritage Corridor Line. It doesn't run on the weekends at all.

The Metra SouthWest Service has a nearby stop in Palos Park. It's just a little over one mile from the entry to Paddock Woods, which grants hikers access to over thirty miles of trails found within these park systems. This would be a great option except, again, the trains are limited on the weekends. There is some service back into Chicago on Saturday and none on Sunday.

As a result, this isn't a good weekend hiking option

for most people. Metra is the umbrella organization for a patchwork of railroads and jurisdictions. It owns some of its tracks, rights, and equipment, but not all of it, and the patchwork around the Palos system has resulted in this very limited train schedule. It's not impossible that in the future that would change, and weekend service could be added, but right now it's not likely.

My goal with this guide is to give every Chicagoan the tools they need to get outside when they can. I'd like to recommend the Palos Trail System to everyone, especially families (there are two nature centers here!) but if you can't get home at the end of the day, I can't recommend you go in the first place. But if trains ran more frequently, this would easily be my number one recommendation for hikers of all abilities and ages.

I have left it in because I think it's demonstrates what we could have, less than sixty minutes from downtown Chicago, with increased access to passenger rail services. The trail system is an unrivaled opportunity for Chicago-area backpackers, bike campers, and big adventure hikers, but the barrier to entry is high. To really make use of this place without a car, today, you need to be able to hike at minimum seven miles and stay at least three nights. That said ....

Suggested itinerary for big adventure hikers, backpackers, bikepackers, and long weekend warriors:

Friday: Catch the SouthWest Service towards Manhattan. This train stops at Palos Park several times throughout the afternoon but try and catch an earlier one if you can, to avoid hiking after dark.

Exit the station and navigate your way to the Sag Valley Trail system. When you arrive at the yellow trail, take a right and follow the north end of the loop. When the yellow loop intersects with the purple Cal-Sag Trail take another right and head north across the river and around Saganashkee Slough. Follow the road straight until about Joe's Pond and take the green path to the right until it comes to the yellow path. Take the yellow path to the left, through Pulaski Woods. When it intersects with the orange path, take that to the left and follow it around Tomahawk Slough. Camp Bullfrog Lake will be ahead of you. Camp here for the weekend.

Miles to Camp Bullfrog Lake from Palos Park Metra: About seven.

Saturday–Sunday: Camp Bullfrog Lake is your base of operations. Enjoy the thirty miles of hiking, fishing, biking, camping, nature centers, lakes, and rivers that can be found here. Check out Swallow Cliff Woods if you're into hiking up steep slopes. Visit Little Red Schoolhouse for interpretive information and a little local history. Visit the Sag Quarries, the I&M Canal, Buffalo Woods, Morrill Meadow Flying Field, and at least three different fens and one canyon. Build a campfire, make s'mores, tell scary stories. Go to bed early Sunday night, because you've got a bright and early morning tomorrow.

Monday: Break camp in the early morning. Exit Camp Bullfrog Lake by taking the yellow path northeast. Continue following it, sticking to the left-hand path. When you come to the parking lot for Willow Springs Woods, exit the park. The Willow Springs Metra will be directly ahead of you. On weekdays the Heritage Corridor Line makes stops at Willow Springs heading into Chicago at 6:13 a.m., 6:55 a.m. and 7:36 a.m. so don't be late.

Miles from Camp Bullfrog Lake to Willow Springs Metra: About three.

On the train home consider how much more useful this park system would be if you could only get to and from it more easily without a car.

Park name	The Palos Trail System
Train station	Palos Park, Palos Heights, and Western Springs
Train line	Metra: SouthWest Service and Heritage Corridor
Schedule	Monday–Friday: departs Chicago as early as 6:26 a.m. and departs Palos Park as late as 10:01 p.m Saturday: departs Chicago as early as 1:30 p.m. and Palos Park as late as 3:45 p.m. No service on Sunday.
Departs from	Union Station
Round-trip travel costs	$13.50 full fare, $6.75 reduced
Entrance	From the Willow Springs Metra station take a left and walk one block down Flavin Rd., the entrance to the park will be directly ahead of you. From the Palos Park Metra station head northwest towards 121st St., turn left. cross the road and follow South Timberlane Dr./Timber Lane north. Take another left onto W. 119th St. and follow the path to the Sag Valley Trail.
Hours	Dawn to dusk
Distance from station to trailhead	About 1 mile
Miles of trails	Over 30
Acres	15,000 acres
Difficulty	★★★★
In-park recreation options	Backpacking, bike packing, fishing, camping, hiking, birding, nature watching, interpretive programs, boating
Amenities	Camp Bullfrog Lake
Safety concerns	The long hike to camp makes this one difficult to access unless you're in good physical condition.

Plants	This area is some of the densest concentration of deep woods you will find in Cook County.
Water	This site includes access to the Des Plaines River, the Sanitary Ship Canal, the Calumet Sag Channel, Tampier Slough, Saganashkee Slough, Bullfrog Lake, Tomahawk Slough, Maple Lake, Longjohn Slough, and a few other, smaller lakes and sloughs.
Geology	The rolling terrain, sloughs, and the Des Plaines River were both shaped by the glaciers, but the canals were man-made over the 19th and 20th centuries.
Accessibility	There are a variety of trails within the Palos Trail System, many are wide flat and paved with crushed gravel and others are roughly maintained, narrow, or over roots and sticks that may cause trip hazards.
Dogs	Yes—on leashes only
Bikes	Yes—this park is very bike-friendly, especially to mountain bikes
Family-friendly	No, because of the lack of access to nearby trains
Nearby restaurants	There is no shortage of bars, restaurants and cafes around the Willow Springs Metra station, the Palos Heights Metra station, and the Palos Park Metra station.

ROCK ISLAND DISTRICT

Blue Island: Cal-Sag Trail

The Cal-Sag Trail is a twenty-six-mile-long path that extends not-quite to the Illinois-Indiana border and goes as far west as Lemont. This multi-use trail travels through some of the south suburbs' most vibrant economic corridors and beautiful natural spaces, and because it runs primarily alongside the Little Calumet River, offers opportunities to view shipping barges floating downriver. This is the longest trail in the southern area of Chicago. Here visitors can access three marinas, three golf courses, and six nature preserves. It connects to the I&M Canal in Lemont, which a very adventurous hiker could take all the way down to LaSalle. The miles this trail traverses cross over some of the best remaining examples of the region's history as a transportation and manufacturing hub of the Rust Belt during the Big Steel era.

A lot of this trail is along roads and streets. It is a designated use path, but it's a good idea to use caution when sharing road space with automobiles. There are wayfinding signs all along the trail, and you can't miss them. These fourteen-foot-tall modular signs are made of steel that becomes stronger as it rusts. Each signpost highlights that community's best assets, and individual supporters.

Take the Cal-Sag Trail to the east for about three miles. Just east of the Joe Louis Golf Course, visitors will come to the Whistler Woods Forest Preserve. Here, they'll find access to the Major Taylor Trail, which runs from here south towards Dan Ryan Woods on paved and off-street paved segments. This eight-mile-long trail is open from sunrise to sunset and has opportunities for biking, hiking, walking, and cross-country skiing.

If instead of heading east, you head west you can ride the Cal-Sag Trail all the way into the Palos Trail system. At 127th St., leave the trail and head south on Central Ave. The Elizabeth A. Conkey Forest Preserve will be directly ahead of you. Here you can explore Rubio Woods and Bur Oak Woods, and camp for the evening at Camp Sullivan. (Check out the Oak Forest Metra station entry for detailed information about this hike.)

If instead you continue westward to the end of the trail, you will enter the Palos Trail system. (See the Big Palos Adventure Camp entry for detailed information on this hike.) Hikers on this trail will access the Palos system at Paddock Woods. If the ten-mile hike from Blue Island's Metra station to the Palos Trail system was enough for you, catch the SouthWest Service line at Palos Heights, and ride back into Chicago. If you're just feeling nice and warmed up, continue on the trail to Camp Bullfrog Lake and camp for the night.

Park name	Cal-Sag Trail
Train station	Blue Island
Train line	Metra: Metra Electric District, Rock Island District
Schedule	Metra Electric: Monday–Friday departs downtown as early as 5:15 a.m. and departs Blue Island as late as 7:41 p.m. Saturday: departs downtown as early as 4:40 a.m. and departs Blue Island as late as 3:08 p.m. Metra Electric District has no service to or from Blue Island on Sundays. Rock Island District: Monday–Friday: departs downtown as early as 6:23 a.m. and departs Blue Island as late as 10:26 P.M. Saturday–Sunday: departs downtown as early as 8:30 a.m. and departs Blue Island as late as 11:01 p.m.
Round-trip travel costs	Metra Electric and Rock Island: $12.50 full fare, $6.25 reduced

Entrance	When you exit the Metra station at Vermont St. you are already on the Cal-Sag Trail. Head south on Chatham St. and cross to the other side of the river, to access the eastern half of the trail, which ends at the Calumet City Prairie and Marsh Nature Preserve 8 miles to the east. To access the western part of the trail from the Blue Island Metra Station exit at Vermont St. and take a left to go west.
Hours	Sunrise to sunset
Distance from station to trailhead	The Cal-Sag Trail runs directly past the Blue Island Metra station, making it one of the easier to access trails from the train.
Miles of trails	26
Acres	About 875 acres of park space in Whistler Woods Forest Preserve, Calumet Woods, and Kickapoo Meadows, which can all be accessed from or near the Cal-Sag Trail just south and west of the Blue Island Metra station.
Difficulty	★★
In-park recreation options	Hiking, biking, canoeing, kayaking, barge watching, fishing
Amenities	Picnic shelters, portable restrooms, bike rentals
Safety concerns	The risk here is to the rivers themselves. Over the last 150 years industry has actively damaged the river and it parts of it have been declared national disaster areas.
Plants	This trail runs alongside the Cal-Sag Channel, which has been improved with the addition of native plants and the removal of invasive plants including buckthorn.
Water	The Cal-Sag Channel on the west and the Little Calumet River on the east.
Geology	Before we altered the Little Calumet River it flowed westward from LaPorte County, Indiana, and made a hairpin turn at what is now Blue Island.

Accessibility	The trail is wide, largely flat without many steep grades and often paved. It is popular with bikers.
Dogs	Yes—on leashes only
Bikes	Yes—this park is very bike friendly
Family-friendly	This is a great option for families on bikes, but traffic may be too busy for hiking with small kiddos.
Nearby restaurants	Blue Island has excellent cafes, bars, taverns, and breweries.

Oak Forest: Midlothian Meadows and Oak Forest Heritage Preserve

There are a few truly great hikes you can take from the Oak Forest Metra station. If you're feeling super adventurous, you might want to see how many of these you can accomplish in one day, but honestly this area is rich in native landscapes and is worth a repeat visit. These trails are considered part of the Tinley Creek trail system and all colors mentioned correspond to the colors designed for each path within that trail system.

Midlothian Meadows

Midlothian Meadows has about two miles of trails that tour the prairies supported by the Midlothian Creek. This looped path is a serene tour through meadows, prairies, and woodlands. It's popular with migrating birds during the spring and fall migration seasons.

Oak Forest Heritage Preserve

As you exit Midlothian Meadows head south across 159th St. Follow the path around the Oak Forest Health Center and you will enter the Oak Forest Heritage Preserve. This forested area includes over two miles of trails and is popular with birders and wildlife watchers. This park sits on a glacial moraine, and the land historically was inhabited by American Indians; archeologists have uncovered at least eight houses and mapped an entire village that existed here in the late seventeenth century. Follow the loop around and return to 159th St., turn left towards South Cicero Ave. to return to the Oak Forest Metra station.

Park name	Midlothian Meadows and Oak Forest Heritage Preserve
Train station	Oak Forest
Train line	Metra: Rock Island District
Schedule	Monday–Friday: departs Chicago as early as 6:23 a.m. and departs Oak Forest as late as 10:11 p.m. Saturday-Sunday: departs Chicago as early as 8:30 a.m. and departs Oak Forest as late as 10:51 p.m.
Departs from	La Salle Street
Round-trip travel costs	$13.50 full fare, $6.75 reduced
Entrance	From the Oak Forest Metra station head south towards 159th St., cross Cicero Ave. and the entrance to the park will be directly ahead of you.
Hours	Sunrise to sunset
Distance from station to trailhead	Less than 1 block
Miles of trails	About 4.5
Acres	About 645
Difficulty	★★
In-park recreation options	Model boating (Midlothian Reservoir), hiking, cross-country skiing, biking, fishing, birding, golfing
Amenities	Few aside from restrooms in Bremen Grove and at the George W. Dunne National Golf Course and Driving Range
Safety concerns	Ticks can be a concern year-round. Trails can become mushy following wet weather.

Plants	Midlothian Meadows has gently rolling hills through prairies, forests, wetlands and ravines. The area surrounding Camp Sullivan is set inside a beautiful oak woodland.
Water	Tinley Creek flows through much of the woodland surrounding Bachelor's Grove. Midlothian Reservoir is on a lower floodplain and can become mushy if weather has been wet.
Accessibility	Many of these trails are wide, largely flat, and without steep grade changes, and paved in crushed stone. Camp Sullivan has an accessible indoor bathroom; the bunkhouses have accessible restrooms including shower, sink, and toilet.
Admission	Depending on the time of year a site at Camp Sullivan can be as low as $21 per night or as high as $36 per night for Cook County residents. Bunkhouses and electric sites go for more.
Dogs	Yes—there is an off-leash dog area at Bremen Grove.
Bikes	Yes—these parks are very bike friendly
Family-friendly	Midlothian Meadows is a very family friendly hike.
Nearby restaurants	Restaurants are clustered around 159th St. and along Cicero Ave.

Oak Forest: Midlothian Reservoir, St. Mihiel Woods, East Yankee Woods, and the George W. Dunne National Golf Course

Midlothian Reservoir

Midlothian Reservoir has about two miles of trails, with places to fish or sail your model boat. Follow the path south past the reservoir and take a left continuing on the path parallel to 167th St. Eventually the trail will intersect with the trail for Tinley Creek; take a hard right and follow it north into the park. The trail is an out-and-back loop, so you will return to this spot at the end.

St. Mihiel Woods East and Yankee Woods

When you exit Midlothian Reservoir's trail, if you cross 167th St. you'll already be at the trailhead for St. Mihiel Woods East. This loop is a little hillier and more difficult than the previous trails outlined, but shorter, with a little over one mile of trail available. As you exit the park, take a left and enjoy a short jaunt through Yankee Woods. Return to the Oak Forest Metra station by heading east on 167th until you arrive at South Cicero Ave., then take a left and follow it north to the train station.

George W. Dunne National Golf Course

From the Oak Forest Metra station head southwest until you come to 159th St. and take a right. Follow it until you come to Central Ave., and the golf course will be ahead. This public golf course has been recognized as one of the top courses to play. It's been praised by golfers who don't see a single building or house across all eighteen holes. The course has been certified as a Cooperative Sanctuary by Audubon International. If you're not a golfer, the course has a three-mile walking path around the course, and a trail through Bremen Grove is accessible from the south end of the park.

Park name	Midlothian Reservoir, St. Mihiel Woods East, Yankee Woods, and the George W. Dunne National Golf Course
Train station	Oak Forest
Train line	Metra: Rock Island District
Schedule	Monday–Friday: departs Chicago as early as 6:23 a.m. and departs Oak Forest as late as 10:11 p.m. Saturday–Sunday: departs Chicago as early as 8:30 a.m. and departs Oak Forest as late as 10:51 p.m.
Departs from	La Salle Street
Round-trip travel costs	$13.50 full fare, $6.75 reduced
Entrance	From the Oak Forest Metra station head southwest towards 163rd St. and turn left onto Oak Ave. The park will be directly ahead of you.
Hours	Sunrise to sunset
Distance from station to trailhead	Midlothian Reservoir: Less than .25 miles
Miles of trails	About 9.5
Acres	About 1,300 acres
Difficulty	★★★
In-park recreation options	Hiking, cross-country skiing, biking, fishing, birding, golfing

Amenities	Few aside from restrooms in Bremen Grove and at the George W. Dunne National Golf Course and Driving Range
Safety concerns	Ticks can be a concern year-round. Trails can become mushy following wet weather.
Plants	Open prairies and marshes are abundant here.
Water	Midlothian Reservoir is on a lower floodplain and can become mushy if weather has been wet.
Accessibility	Many of these trails are wide, largely flat, and without steep grade changes, and paved in crushed stone.
Admission	Free, but there is a fee associated with the golf course.
Dogs	Yes—there is an off-leash dog area at Bremen Grove.
Bikes	Yes—these parks are very bike friendly.
Family-friendly	Midlothian Reservoir is a pretty family-friendly hike.
Nearby restaurants	Restaurants are clustered around 159th St. and along Cicero Ave.

Oak Forest: Camp Sullivan and the area around Bachelor's Grove Woods

Adventure-seekers take note: I suggest making this one its own big overnighter.

Camp Sullivan has year-round camping available. Tent campsites can fit up to six people and come with a 10' x 10' mulched tent pad, picnic table, and fire ring. Tent campers might need to walk a little bit from the parking area, but that just means a quieter campsite. Large bunkhouses with space for up to thirty-six people are available, including heat, porch, picnic table, and fire ring. A smaller bunkhouse offers those same amenities for up to sixteen people. The smallest cabins are not heated and has room for up to eight people. There is also a twenty-eight-foot climbing wall inside an activity barn.

If you're not staying the evening at Camp Sullivan, instead follow the Red Trail to the left at the fork. This path is almost ten miles long, so it can be worth it to take your time and stay a day or two. If you tried to do the whole thing in one day, you'd easily put in over seventeen miles. If that sounds like a fun day to you, good luck, my outdoorsy friend. If you walk straight from the Metra station to Camp Sullivan, you'll have put in just under four and a third miles, which for backpacker looking to get out for a weekend just thirty minutes from downtown Chicago, is easy peasy. Bachelor Woods and Burr Oak Woods make up the bulk of this protected space, with Rubio Woods making up a significant additional portion. Here you'll find native plants and wildlife, including the threatened bur oak.

Park name	**Camp Sullivan, Carlson Springs Woods, Rubio Woods, Bachelor's Grove Woods, Elizabeth A. Conkey Forest, North, Arrowhead Lake, Turtlehead Lake, Bur Oak Woods, and Tinley Creek Woods.**
Train station	Oak Forest
Train line	Metra: Rock Island District
Schedule	Monday–Friday: departs Chicago as early as 6:23 a.m. and departs Oak Forest as late as 10:11 p.m. Saturday–Sunday: departs Chicago as early as 8:30 a.m. and departs Oak Forest as late as 10:51 p.m.
Departs from	La Salle Street
Round-trip travel costs	$13.50 full fare, $6.75 reduced
Entrance	From the Oak Forest Metra station head southwest and take a right onto 159th St. Continue straight until you come to the George W. Dunne National Golf Course and pick up the trail there. Follow this until you pass Ridgeland Ave. Cross to the north side of the street and you'll be on the 1.7-mile Green Trail. This will take you north to the Red Trail. Follow the road directly ahead of you instead of choosing either fork of the Red Trail and you will come to Camp Sullivan.
Hours	Sunrise to sunset
Distance from station to trailhead	Camp Sullivan, et al: About 1.25 miles
Miles of trails	About 13.5
Acres	About 4,300
Difficulty	★★★

In-park recreation options	Hiking, cross-country skiing, biking, fishing, birding, golfing
Amenities	Few aside from restrooms in Bremen Grove and at the George W. Dunne National Golf Course and Driving Range
Safety concerns	Ticks can be a concern year-round. Trails can become mushy following wet weather.
Plants	Much of this is set into deep oak woodlands.
Water	Midlothian Reservoir is on a lower floodplain and can become mushy if weather has been wet.
Accessibility	Many of these trails are wide, largely flat and without steep grade changes and paved in crushed stone.
Dogs	Yes—there is an off-leash dog area at Bremen Grove
Bikes	Yes—these parks are very bike friendly
Family-friendly	This hike is a challenge, and young children might find it to be too much.
Nearby restaurants	Restaurants are clustered around 159th St. and along Cicero Ave.

Joliet: Joliet Ironworks Historic Site and the I&M Canal

The Joliet Iron and Steel Works was once the second-largest steel mill in the United States. It operated primarily from 1869 to 1936. Much of the Works closed in the early 1900s, and the Works closed for good in the early 1980s. In 1991, the Forest Preserve District of Will County purchased the site for its historic merit, and it opened to public as a park in 1998. Today park managers are working to reclaim the natural landscape of the area, while respecting the archeological history of the Iron Works site and allowing it to continue to decay naturally. If hikes through industrial ruins sound appealing to you, put this one on your list.

Joliet, which calls itself the City of Steel and Stone, has a long and proud history as one of the biggest steel producers within the Rust Belt, so reclaiming the site along the Des Plaines River made a great deal of sense. Between the thousands of jobs available in the steel industry, and the plentiful nearby quarrying jobs, that's how Joliet got its nickname. Many immigrants from northern and western Europe were able to find good jobs and settle here. Interpretive signage along the path gives a better understanding of who worked at the steel mill, and how it came to shape Joliet and the greater Chicagoland region.

Over the following decades the site continued to decay, and nature took over. By the time it was developed into a public park, it was heavily overgrown with mostly invasive species.

From the Iron Works visitors can travel north and access the Illinois and Michigan Canal (I&M Canal). The I&M Canal's construction connected the East

Coast with the Gulf of Mexico via water, by connecting Lake Michigan to the Mississippi River. This idea was first suggested by French explorers Louis Jolliet and Father Jacques Marquette as far back as the 1680s, but the canal was not completed until 1848. It was a vital resource for shipping and passengers and remained in use until 1933. Nature reclaimed the space until 2003 when it was turned into a park. Today, it's a home for wildlife and recreation.

This section of the I&M is about seven and a half miles long and runs from the Iron Works north through the city of Lockport, ending in Romeoville. The Romeoville entrance is through Isle a la Cache, a 101-acre preserve that is part of the Des Plaines River system, and offers opportunities for hiking, cross-country skiing and snowshoeing, fishing, canoeing, and geocaching. The Isle a la Cache Museum is located here and has historical and interpretive information for kids. It is free and open to the public.

The I&M connects to Veteran's Memorial Trail and the Centennial Trail at Isle a la Cache before continuing further north. Those two trails travel alongside each other until the intersection with I-355, where they split. From there, you can take the Centennial Trail east toward Willow Springs, and Veteran's Memorial north to Woodridge.

This northern stretch is just a short portion of the entire I&M Canal Trail. Although it doesn't connect within Joliet, the I&M has over sixty contiguous miles of crushed gravel trail that an adventurous person could take as far south as LaSalle, Illinois. *Pro tip: When the weather is nice try and count the turtles you see sunning themselves along the canal. I bet you'll run out of fingers to count on pretty quickly.*

Park name	**Joliet Ironworks Historic Site and the I&M Canal**
Train station	Joliet
Train line	Metra: Rock Island Line
Schedule	Monday–Friday: departs Chicago as early as 6:23 a.m. and departs Joliet as late as 9:45 p.m. Saturday–Sunday: departs Chicago as early as 8:30 a.m. and departs Joliet as late as 2 a.m.
Departs from	LaSalle Street
Round-trip travel costs	Full fare $16.50, reduced fare $8.25
Entrance	From the Joliet Metra station head north on Scott St. (IL-53) for about one mile. The entrance will be directly ahead of you.
Hours	8 a.m. to sunset
Distance from station to trailhead	About 1 mile
Miles of trails	About .5 miles in the Ironworks site, which also gives you access to over 7 miles of trail along the Illinois & Michigan Canals.
Acres	Joliet Iron Works: 42 acres I&M Canal: 100 acres
Difficulty	★★
In-park recreation options	Biking, hiking, running, in-line skating (on a 3.26-mile paved segment north of 135th St.), cross-country skiing, snowshoeing
Amenities	Picnic shelters
Safety concerns	Climbing is not allowed on the industrial ruins.
Geology	This site features the foundations of a once-bustling iron and steel factory.

Water	The Des Plaines River runs alongside the Iron Works and the I&M Canal.
Accessibility	The .6-mile interpretive trail is paved. The I&M Canal is wide, flat, and paved with crushed gravel.
Dogs	Yes—on leashes only
Bikes	Yes—this park is very bike friendly
Family-friendly	This is a great option for kids who like to get up close with nature and run off some steam, just remember that climbing the ruins is prohibited.
Nearby restaurants	Restaurants, cafes, and bars are abundant on Chicago St.

SOUTH
SHORE LINE

Dune Park: Indiana Dunes State Park

While Indiana Dunes is one of the country's newest national parks, don't sleep on the state park either. Surrounded by the national park, the state park has beautiful hikes though some gorgeous oak savannahs, leading down to Lake Michigan. If it's a hot summer day, you can swim here. That said, if there are signs posted advising you that conditions are not right for swimming, stay out.

Exit the Dune Park train station and head north for a little less than one mile. There is a designated footpath separated from traffic leading directly into the park. When you enter the park, you will approach the park office, where you can pick up a map and check on trail conditions. From here, you can access the trails, campground, beaches, and shelters. Marshes and dunes are abundant here, and you can see a dune blow out in process by visiting Trail 9. The only way to access the national park from the state park is by taking a long walk along the beach. There are no trails that directly connect the two.

The state park has the surprisingly difficult Three Dune Challenge. This one-and-a-half-mile trail takes you to the top of the three tallest dunes in the park, Mount Jackson (elevation 176 feet), Mount Holden (184 feet), and Mount Tom (192 feet). If that weren't enough, parts of the trail are forty-degree slopes on a trail made of, well, sand. You'll see everyone on this trail, from spandex-outfitted trail runners to troops of Brownies and Boy Scouts. If you go at your own pace, I guarantee you will find this hike challenging and rewarding.

Year-round camping is available in the state park, which is a good option for winter camping when Dunewood Campground is closed. The campground has 138 campsites, all including an electric hookup.

Sites are spacious, but not exactly private. Reservations can be made in advance at camp.IN.gov or 866-622-6746. Up to six adults can stay at a single campsite. The distance from the train station to the campground is a little over two miles, completely separated from traffic.

Park name	Indiana Dunes State Park
Train station	Dune Park
Train line	South Shore Line
Schedule	Daily: from 8:45 a.m. to 12:45 a.m.
Departs from	Millennium Station
Round-trip travel costs	$18 per person round trip; $9 per reduced fare round trip. These tickets must be purchased using the South Shore Line app. Ventra does not work on the South Shore line.
Entrance	Exit the Dune Park station and walk .9 miles north to enter Indiana Dunes State Park.
Hours	Trails 7 a.m. - 11 p.m. (be aware that it can be dangerous hiking on the dunes after dark, use your best judgement.) Nature center: 9:30 a.m. - 4:30 p.m. local time
Distance from station to trailhead	Less than 1 mile
Miles of trails	Indiana Dunes State Park has nearly 17 miles of trails, including the 1.5-mile but surprisingly difficult 3 Dune Challenge.
Acres	Indiana Dunes State Park occupies 2,182 acres along three miles of Lake Michigan's southern shoreline. Next door is Indiana Dunes National Park, which occupies 15,000 acres of dunes, wetlands, prairies, rivers, and forests.
Difficulty	★★★

In-park recreation options	Beachgoing, swimming, biking, hiking, bird watching, camping, fishing, boating, geocaching, historical sites
Amenities	Nature center, picnic shelter, fishing (smelt only), campground
Safety concerns	Lake Michigan can be a fickle thing and can easily become dangerous during rough weather. If access to Lake Michigan has been restricted, please follow those rules.
Plants	The park provides habitat for approximately 1,130 native vascular plants, including the federally threatened Pitcher's thistle. The park is home to huge concentrations of Indiana's listed rare, threatened, endangered, and special concern plant species. Shaped by glacial events and changing climates, the dunes landscape contains flora representative of eastern deciduous forests, boreal forest remnants, and species with Atlantic coast affinities. In addition, the park is part of the upper- and easternmost limits of the tallgrass prairie peninsula and supports high quality remnants of this threatened landscape.
Accessibility	Within the campground, sites 7, 22, 28, 53, 119 and 127 are all accessible. Many of the trails are made of sand and can be difficult to navigate.
Dogs	Dogs are not allowed on the Indiana Dunes State Park beaches. Everywhere else within the park, including the campground, dogs must be on a leash no longer than 6 feet.
Bikes	Bikes are allowed on the roads within the park and are prohibited on trails.
Family-friendly	This is a great option for families with kids of all ages.
Admission	Indiana Dunes State Park charges a fee for all vehicles that enter the park, but not for walk-in visitors.
Nearby restaurants	Not really

Miller, Ogden Dunes, and Beverly Shores: Indiana Dunes National Park and the Dunewood Campground

Indiana Dunes National Park fully surrounds Indiana Dunes State Park. The South Shore Line runs straight through it, with three stops that make it simple to access most of the park. The most notable feature about the Indiana Dunes is, well, the dunes. They are geology happening at a rapid pace, which means conditions on the dunes or the lakefront can change dramatically and quickly. Within the national park's 15,000 acres, visitors will find the fourth most biodiverse park in the national park system, and roughly one-third of all the rare plants that exist within Indiana. If you like the feeling of sand between your toes, put this one on your list. Often during the warmer months, the national park service will operate shuttle services within the park, including from the Dunewood Campground to other locations within the park. Check with the NPS for current schedule information.

Miller:

This station is the closest one to Chicago, but it's a little far from the beach. That said, it is the easiest way to access the Paul H. Douglas Center for Environmental Education. This nature center has interpretive programming, information about the park and the natural landscape and interactive exhibits. Stop here and pick up a map and brochure before heading to explore the trails. The Miller Woods Trail traverses wetlands, a globally rare black oak savannah, dunes, and a beach. The savannah is particularly beautiful during the springtime when wildflowers color the landscape, including wild lupines. The lupines are the only food that the endangered karner blue butterfly can eat, so it is possible to spot them during the warmer months. The trail is narrow, and walkers must stay single-file to avoid trampling this rare habitat. Also, there's poison ivy, so you really do want to stay on the trail.

Ogden Dunes:

From the Ogden Dunes station, it's a little trickier to access the beach. Thankfully, it's very easy to access the stunning Tolleston Dunes Trail. The Tolleston Dunes Trail, almost three miles long, takes visitors through 4,700-year-old sand dunes that were formed when Lake Michigan's water level was at least twenty-five feet higher than today. In its previous life, this site was a sand mining operation, which is why the parking lot and the area around that are so flat. Overall the trail sees roughly 127 feet of elevation gain, with grades between two and nine percent. This makes it the second youngest dune system within the national park, and it gives us an idea of what life was like before Lake Michigan's shoreline changed so dramatically. Here visitors will find oak savannah habitats and wetlands. Keep an eye out for the prickly pear cactus, which yes, does grow here in the Midwest. Bikes are not permitted within this trail system. The marsh overlook is wheelchair accessible, but the trail is not.

Beverly Shores:

Just a short five-minute walk from the Metra station at Beverly Shores you'll come to the Dunewood Campground. For the transit-adjacent backpacker looking to do a quick overnight in the Chicago region this is pretty much the ideal close-to-home setup. It's just close enough to town that you can pick up anything you forgot and far enough away from the city to feel like you got away.

This campground is tucked into an oak forest, and only about one mile on foot from Lake Michigan. Sites are spaced reasonably far apart to provide some privacy. Firewood is for sale just outside of the campground entrance.

Many sites are reservable online starting six months in advance of the check-in date. Sites are reservable beginning November 15 for the following camping season. Some of the walk-in sites are first-come, first-served, and offer greater privacy, with no cars in sight. All sites are paid for at the campground entrance automated kiosk. Sites 1-54 are conventional drive-in sites for RVs and/or tents. RV length is limited in some sites. Sites 55-67 are walk-in sites for tent camping only. Bicycles must remain on paved roads in this campground and campfires must be within the provided grates.

From Dunewood Campground it's easy to access several hiking and biking trails, including the Great Marsh Trail, the Calumet Bike Trail, the Dunewood Trace, and the Calumet Dune Trail. Walk straight north on Broadway and you will come to a swimming beach directly on Lake Michigan.

From this spot, if you head further east along the coastline, you will come to Mount Baldy, which rises 126 feet above Lake Michigan. While generally Indiana Dunes National Park is a very safe place to visit, access to Mount Baldy's summit is restricted. Authorized ranger-led daytime and sunset hikes occur on weekends during the summer. Why? To make a long story short, over the course of the last century Mount Baldy has been moving inland. When this process started there was a mature oak forest behind the dune. When it moved, it overtook the mature oak forest. In 2013 a family was on vacation at the park and hiked to the summit of the dune. The son, then five years old, was briefly unsupervised when he found a hole in the top of the dune and climbed into it. The entrance to the hole then disappeared when the sand covered it up, with the boy inside. This set off a nearly four-hour-long rescue operation that resulted in the child being rescued, miraculously alive, twelve feet beneath the surface of the dune.

So, what happened? Scientists have determined that over the last century that mature oak forest began to decay beneath the sand. When Mount Baldy was in a different place, the tops of the old trees were buried under twenty feet of sand. Today, the tops of those trees are near the summit of Mount Baldy, and while the trees have decayed within the dune, their structures have not collapsed. Basically, the boy became trapped inside the trunk of a hollowed-out oak tree that was swallowed up by a sand dune over the course of decades. So please, stay off the summit of Mount Baldy unless on a ranger-guided hike. That said, the nearby Beach Trail is a short, steep climb up loose sand leading to the beach and that is open and unrestricted.

Back at the intersection, if instead of turning east towards Mount Baldy, you turn west and follow the coast you will come across houses that were relocated here following the 1933 Century of Progress World's Fair. The houses were built to demonstrate the kind of homes we thought people would be living in by the twenty-first-century, and in many ways these houses are still very futuristic. The houses are currently owned by Landmarks Indiana, which leased them to the National Park Service, which sub-leased them to individuals to live in and restore them in exchange for long-term leases. Continue west along the shoreline and you will enter Indiana Dunes State Park.

Park name	Indiana Dunes National Park
Train station	Miller: closest to the Paul H. Douglas Center for Environmental Education and Miller Woods Trail Ogden Dunes: nearest to West Beach, Portage Lakefront, and Riverwalk Beverly Shores: nearest to Dunewood Campground
Train line	South Shore Line
Schedule	Daily from 8:45 a.m. to 12:45 a.m.,
Departs from	Millennium Station
Round-trip travel costs	Miller: $15 per person round trip, $7.50 reduced Ogden Dunes and Beverly Shores: $18 per person round trip; $9 per reduced fare round trip
Entrance	Miller: From the Miller Metra station head east towards Lake Street. Take a right and head north towards the Paul H. Douglas Center for Environmental Education. The trail starts here. Ogden Dunes: From the Ogden Dunes station head west on Dunes Highway until you see the entrance for the Inland Marsh Trail and Tolleston dunes. This route is short, but it does not have a sidewalk. There is a wide shoulder along the two-lane road so please use caution when walking down the side of it. Beverly Shores: After exiting the Beverly Shores station walk south on Broadway until you find the trailhead.
Hours	Park areas are open from 6 a.m.-11 p.m., Central Time
Camp-ground open	April through October
Distance from station to trailhead	Miller: About .75 miles Ogden Dunes: About .25 miles Beverly Shores: About .25 miles

Miles of trails	Indiana Dunes National Park has more than 50 miles of trails on 14 distinct trail systems.
Acres	Indiana Dunes National Park occupies 15,000 acres of dunes, wetlands, prairies, rivers, and forests.
Difficulty	★★–★★★
In-park recreation options	Beachgoing, swimming, biking, hiking, bird watching, camping, fishing, boating, geocaching, historical sites
Amenities	Restrooms and showers are in the center of each loop. No electric or water hookups at individual sites. There is potable water located at several locations in each loop.
Safety concerns	Ticks have become a year-round concern in the region and the National Park Service advises performing a thorough tick check after leaving the park. The summit of Mount Baldy is closed to visitors except during ranger-led hikes that occur on weekends during the summer.
Plants	Indiana Dunes is full of oak and hickory trees. This park has more than 1,400 species of vascular plants, putting it eighth in total plant species among all national parks. Indiana Dunes National Park is the fourth most biodiverse national park. The Pinhook Bog has roughly one-third of the rare plants in the entire state of Indiana, including pink lady's slippers, an orchid native to the region.
Water	Lake Michigan's shoreline includes soft beaches, and sand dunes. On a relatively clear day it's easy to view the Chicago skyline from the shore. Lake Michigan can become dangerous during rough weather, so check with the Park Service regarding daily lake conditions.
Geology	Indiana Dunes has some of the tallest dunes created by a lake in the world.

Accessibility	Inside the Dunewood Campground sites 15, 30, 41, and 55 are wheelchair accessible. There are accessible beach overlooks at the Portage Lake Front, Lake View Beach, and Porter Beach. The Calumet Trail is ADA-compliant. Depending on the conditions in Lake Michigan there may be an accessible beach walk. Some sand-capable wheelchairs are available to borrow from the Park Service at no cost. This is a first-come, first-served amenity so call ahead to verify availability. The Paul H. Douglas Environmental Center is fully accessible.
Admission	The campground has a $25 per night camping fee. There is no entrance fee for the park itself.
Dogs	Dogs are allowed but must be kept on a leash no longer than 6 feet. Dogs are not allowed near the lifeguard area at West Beach, the equestrian trails or Pinhook Bog.
Bikes	In the campground bikes can be walked to the walk-in sites. There are bike-friendly trails throughout the national park, but bikes are not welcome in most of the state park.
Family-friendly	This is a great option for getting families with kids of all ages into nature overnight.
Nearby restaurants	Near Beverly Shores, just around the corner from Dunewood Campground there is a cafe, market, and pub called Goblin & The Grocer. There is also Camp Stop General Store & Beach Shop, where you can pick up supplies.

Suggested Itineraries

FOR ADVENTURE SEEKERS
- The Big Palos Adventure Hike
- Camp Sullivan
- Des Plaines River Trail
- Deer Park (Camp Reinberg)

FOR STROLLER FAMILIES
- Round Lake–Hart's Woods Park and Nippersink Forest Preserve
- Itasca–Springbrook Nature Center and Songbird Slough
- Garfield Park Conservatory
- Woodstock–Emricson Park and Ryder's Woods

FOR THE SOCIAL MEDIA-INCLINED
- Cuba Marsh Forest Preserve
- Schiller Park
- Geneva–Fox River Trail
- The Chicago Botanic Garden

FOR QUICK TRIPS
- Garfield Park Conservatory
- Northerly Island Park
- LaBagh Woods
- Fort Sheridan Nature Preserve

FOR SPRING HIKES
- Indiana Dunes National Park (Tolleston Dunes Trail)

- Joliet Iron Works and the I&M Canal
- Baker's Lake Nature Preserve
- The 606 and the Bloomingdale Trail

FOR SUMMER HIKES
- Indiana Dunes State Park
- Illinois Beach State Park
- The Lakefront Trail
- Fort Sheridan Nature Preserve

FOR FALL HIKES
- Ryder's Woods Park
- Deer Grove Forest Preserve
- Veteran's Acres and Sterne's Woods & Fen
- Elburn Forest Preserve

FOR WINTER HIKES
- Garfield Park Conservatory
- LaBagh Woods
- Somme Preserves
- Thatcher Woods

CAMPGROUNDS
- Illinois Beach State Park
- Indiana Dunes National Park–Dunewood Campground
- Indiana Dunes State Park
- Camp Bullfrog Lake–The Big Palos Adventure Hike
- Camp Sullivan–Oak Forest
- Camp Reinberg–Palatine

Acknowledgements

This book could not have been completed without the help of the following:

The Chicago Transit Authority and Metra, without whom we would all be stuck in traffic; Carl Vogel and the dedicated team that run and maintain the Cook County Forest Preserves; the Round Lake Park District and the team at the Prairie Grass Nature Museum; John Fiorina and the whole staff at the Crystal Lake Nature Center; Chris Lynk with Woodstock Recreation District; Land Conservancy of McHenry County; Itasca Park District; Forest Preserves of DuPage County; Laurie Metanchuk with the Forest Preserve District of Kane County; Geneva Park District; Western Springs Park District; Friends of the Cal-Sag Trail; Indiana Dunes State Park; the Illinois Department of Natural Resources; Eriko Kojima, volunteer steward at the Somme Preserves; Lake County Forest Preserve District; and Ranger Rafi Wilkinson of the National Park Service.

JUL - - 2020